Nick Vandome

Android Phones
for Seniors

2nd edition
Illustrated using Android 7.0 Nougat

In easy steps is an imprint of In Easy Steps Limited
16 Hamilton Terrace · Holly Walk · Leamington Spa
Warwickshire · United Kingdom · CV32 4LY
www.ineasysteps.com

Second Edition

In Easy Steps Limited supports The Forest Stewardship Council (FSC),
the leading international forest certification organization. All our titles
that are printed on Greenpeace approved FSC certified paper carry the
FSC logo.

MIX
Paper from
responsible sources
FSC® C020837

Printed and bound in the United Kingdom

ISBN 978-1-84078-874-7

Contents

4   Around an Android Phone   55

5   Calls and Contacts   83

1 Introducing Android Phones

Smartphones using the Android operating system are the most used phones, worldwide. This chapter gives an overview of Android on a smartphone. It also looks at creating a Google Account for using Google services on your Android smartphone.

About Android

Android is essentially a mobile computing operating system – i.e. one for mobile devices such as smartphones and tablets.

Android is an open source operating system, which means that the source code is made available to hardware manufacturers and developers so that they can design their devices and apps in conjunction with Android. This has created a large community of Android developers, and also means that Android is not tied to one specific device; individual manufacturers can use it (as long as they meet certain specific criteria), which leads to Android being available on a variety of different devices.

Android is based on the flexible and robust Linux operating system and shares many similarities with it.

Android Inc. was founded in 2003, and the eponymous operating system was initially developed for mobile devices. Google quickly saw this as an opportunity to enter the smartphone and tablet market and bought Android in 2005. The first Android-powered smartphone appeared in 2008 and since then has gone from strength to strength. Android-based smartphones have a majority of the worldwide market, and it is used by numerous manufacturers on their handsets.

The main differences between the Android mobile operating system and desktop- or laptop-based ones such as Windows or macOS are:

- **No file structure**. There is no default built-in file manager structure for storing and managing files. All content is saved within the app in which it is created.

- **Self-contained apps**. Because there is no file structure, apps are generally self-contained and do not communicate with each other, unless required.

- **Numerous Home screens**. There are numerous Home screens on an Android phone, and they can be used to store and access apps.

- Generally, **content is saved automatically as it is created**. Apps save content as it is created, so there is no Save or Save As function within many apps.

The New icon pictured above indicates a new or enhanced feature introduced with Android phones using Android 7.0 Nougat.

About Android Phones

Android has been used on smartphones since 2008. Initially adoption was fairly slow, but this has now accelerated to the point where Android is the most widely used operating system on smartphones.

Combinations of Android phones

Since Android can be used by different manufacturers, this means that a range of the latest smartphones always run on Android. In addition, since not all older phones are designed to be upgraded to the latest version of Android, there are phones running several different versions of Android – for instance, the Google Pixel 3 runs the latest version of Android (at the time of printing, Android 9 Pie), while some models of older phones may still only be able to run Android 4.3 Jelly Bean. As a result, there are hundreds of combinations in terms of smartphone models and versions of Android on the market. Some are the expensive flagship models, which will run a relatively new version of Android (although not necessarily the very latest version) compared with cheaper models that can only run an older version of Android.

Checking for versions of Android

When buying an Android phone, look at the version of Android in the phone's specification. Ideally, it should be a relatively new version, in order to enable it to be upgraded to the latest version when it becomes available. Some models of Android phones reach a point where they do not have the required hardware to update to the next version of Android and are therefore stuck with the current version that they are using. This may also limit the phone's ability to download and use the latest apps that are available.

Android phone differences

Despite the variations in versions of Android, the user experience is generally the same on different Android phones. However, one area of difference is the hardware used by manufacturers. For instance, some newer Android phones have fingerprint sensors for unlocking the phone, and others have more sophisticated cameras.

Updated versions of Android are named alphabetically after items of confectionery.

Due to the range of versions of Android on smartphones, it is not feasible to cover all possibilities across different manufacturers. Therefore, this book will focus on the standard functionality of Android that is available through all versions of the operating system. It will feature Android version 7.0 Nougat, which is the version of Android most widely adopted on Android phones (at the time of printing). The examples will also be from a Samsung phone, one of the most widely used brands of smartphone on the market.

Updating Android

Since Android is open source and can be used on a variety of different devices, this can sometimes cause delays in updating the operating system on the full range of eligible Android devices. This is because it has to be tailored specifically for each different device; it is not a case of "one size fits all". This can lead to delays in the latest version being rolled out to all compatible devices. The product cycle for new versions is usually six to nine months.

As Android is a Google product, Google's own devices are usually the first ones to run the latest version of the software. Therefore, the Google Pixel 3 was the first phone to run the latest version of Android, 9.0 Pie, while others are still running previous versions, such as 4.4 KitKat, 5.0 Lollipop, 6.0 Marshmallow, 7.0 Nougat or 8.0 Oreo. For recently released phones, an upgrade to the latest version of Android will be scheduled into the update calendar or it might be already available to install. However, for some older Android phones the latest version of the software is not always made available. This can be because of hardware limitations, but there have also been suggestions that it is a move by hardware manufacturers designed to ensure that consumers upgrade to the latest products.

The version of the Android operating system that is being used on your phone can be viewed from within the **About device** section of the **Settings** app. This is where details of the current version of Android can be viewed (in the Software Info section).

Much of the general functionality of the Android operating system is the same, regardless of the version being used.

For more details about the Android settings, see Chapter Three.

Settings

SOFTWARE INFO

Android version
7.0

Baseband version
G920FXXU5EQCD

Kernel version
3.10.61-10958180
dpi@SWHE0306 #1
Tue Jul 4 19:45:39 KST 2017

Build number
NRD90M.G920FXXS5EQG1

SE for Android status
Enforcing
SEPF_SECMOBILE_7.0_0005
Tue Jul 04 20:04:08 2017

97% 17:09

Android Overlays

Because Android is an open source operating system, it means that manufacturers can amend it, to a certain extent, when they add it to their phone models. This keeps the core Android operating system, but the user interface can be adapted so that it becomes specific to each manufacturer. This is known as an "overlay" and means that the appearance of Android will be different on, for instance, a Samsung phone and an HTC one. However, the operation of Android will still be the same on different brands of phones and, in most cases, the appearance of the user interface will be very similar and still recognizable as Android.

Beware

If you are familiar with one brand of Android phone and then switch to another, it may take a little while to get used to the overlay of the new phone. However, the underlying functionality should be the same.

In addition to overlays, manufacturers can also add their own apps to their brand of Android phone and, in some cases, have their own app store for downloading more apps.

The one phone that does not have any kind of overlay is the Google Pixel 3: since Google own Android, they use the operating system in its purest form on their phones.

Features of Android 8.0

Although Android 8.0 Oreo is a newer version than 7.0 Nougat, it is only available on a limited number of Android phones and version 7.0 has a higher adoption rate. The majority of features are the same as for earlier versions of Android. However, some of the new features include:

2x faster booting up
Depending on your handset, Android 8.0 Oreo can be two times faster at booting up when turned on.

Notification dots
When there are notifications for apps in Android 8.0 Oreo, a dot appears on the app. This displays the number of notifications that are available. Press on the app to view the notifications and action them as required.

Notification snoozing
One of the options for notifications in Android 8.0 Oreo is for snoozing them, so that you can view them at a later time.

Picture-in-Picture
Android 8.0 Oreo supports Picture-in-Picture, which means that a thumbnail of a video can be displayed in the bottom right-hand corner while you are viewing something else in the main part of the screen.

Nested settings
The settings have been refined in Android 8.0 Oreo, so that more of them are included as nested settings under a main heading. Click on the main heading to view the items that are nested within it.

Battery-saving features
Android 8.0 Oreo has built-in battery-saving features, such as limiting the number of times that an app can request a location or look for updates in the background.

Wi-Fi connection
This can be used to connect to a Wi-Fi network automatically, if you have previously connected to it.

Features of Android 9.0

The latest version of Android (at the time of printing) is Android 9.0 Pie, which is only available on a limited number of Android phones. The majority of features are the same as for earlier versions of Android. However, some of the new features include:

Gesture navigation
Android 9.0 Pie is the first version of Android to enable gesture navigation on the screen, rather than relying on the standard three-button navigation system (Recent items, Home and Back) that has been used with numerous versions of Android. Now, with compatible devices, gestures on the screen can be used to perform a number of tasks. These include: tapping the new Home icon to return to the Home screen; swiping up from the middle-bottom of the screen to access the Recent items of recently used apps; and swiping up twice from the middle-bottom of the screen to access the app drawer to quickly open more apps.

Adaptive battery
This is a feature aimed at saving battery power through Android learning about which apps you use the most and then adjusting the function of less frequently used apps accordingly. The adaptive battery function can be turned on in **Settings** > **Battery** > **Adaptive Battery**.

App actions
This is a feature whereby Google apps can be launched depending on your location – e.g. a shortcut to the Maps app can appear when you leave home.

Dark mode
This can be used to actively select Dark mode, whereby the background on the phone becomes black.

Security features
Android 9.0 Pie contains a number of security updates that are not immediately obvious. Some of them consist of restricting access to your phone while apps are not being used, so that they can only have access when they are active.

The traditional Android buttons can still be used on phones that support gesture navigation.

Features of Android Phones

The button for turning a phone on and off is located on the side of the body of the device in most cases, as are the other buttons and ports that can be used for various functions on your phone.

On/Off button. This can also be used to put the phone into Sleep mode. Press and hold for a couple of seconds to turn on the phone. Press once to put it to sleep or wake it up from sleep.

If the Android operating system is updated on a phone, it will probably restart before the update takes effect.

Turning off. To turn off an Android phone, press and hold on the On/Off button until the **Power off** button appears on the screen. Tap on this to turn the phone off. Tap on **Restart** to shut down the phone and then start it again.

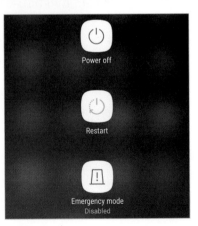

Volume button. This is either a single button on the opposite side to the On/Off button, or two separate buttons. Press the buttons to adjust the volume.

Cameras. There is the main, rear-facing camera (on the back of the phone) for taking pictures. Most phones also have a front-facing camera (on the screen side of the phone), which is usually a lower resolution and is useful for making video calls or taking "selfies", as the user can view the screen at the same time as using the camera.

"Selfies" are photos taken of yourself, using the front-facing camera (on the screen of the phone).

Headphone jack. This is used to connect a headphone cable, and is usually at the top or bottom of the phone.

Micro USB port. This can be used to attach the phone to an adapter for charging the phone, or to a computer for charging or to download content from (or upload to) the phone, using the supplied USB cable. Once the phone is connected to a computer it will show up as a removable drive in the file manager, in the same way as an item such as a flashdrive.

An increasing number of phones, particularly the higher-end models, have a fingerprint sensor on the body of the phone that can be used to unlock the phone with a unique fingerprint. Fingerprint sensors have to be set up by using the applicable item (usually in the Settings app) and then pressing on the sensor several times so that it can identify your unique fingerprint. More than one fingerprint can usually be set up for use with the sensor.

microSD cards. These can be inserted into the appropriate slot on the body of the phone to increase the amount of storage for items such as photos and music.

15

SIM cards usually use 3G, 4G or 5G networks for providing cellular phone and data services – e.g. texting and messaging. 5G is the fastest, but not currently as widely available as 3G and 4G. The G in the name stands for Generation.

Don't forget

Some Android phones, particularly older models, have the SIM tray located inside the phone and this can be accessed by removing the back panel of the phone. The battery can also be located here in Android phones where the SIM is accessed in this way.

SIM Cards

The SIM card for your Android phone will be provided by your mobile carrier – i.e. the company that provides your cellular phone and data services. Without this, you would still be able to communicate using your phone, but only via Wi-Fi and compatible services. A SIM card gives you access to a mobile network too. Newer Android phones have a slot on the side (a SIM tray) for inserting a SIM card. To insert a SIM card into the side SIM tray:

1 The SIM tray is located on the side of the phone, with a small hole at the end of it

2 Use the SIM tool (that should be provided with the phone) to open the SIM tray, by pressing firmly into the hole in Step 1

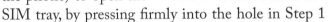

3 Pull out the SIM tray and remove it fully from the phone

4 Insert the SIM card into the SIM tray and return it into the slot in the phone

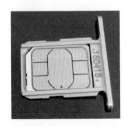

Setting Up Your Phone

When you first turn on your phone (by pressing and holding the On/Off button) you will be taken through the setup process. This only has to be done once, and some of the steps can be completed or amended at a later time, usually within the **Settings** app. Some of the elements that can be applied during the setup process include:

- **Language**. This option lets you select the language to use for your phone. Whichever language is selected will affect all of the system text on the phone, and it will also apply to all user accounts on the phone.

- **Wi-Fi**. This can be used to set up your Wi-Fi so that you can access the web and online services. In the **Select Wi-Fi** window, tap on the name of your router. Enter the password for your router and tap on the **Connect** button.

- **Google Account**. At this stage you can create a Google Account, or sign in with an existing one. Once you have done this, you will have full access to the Google Account services and you will not have to enter your login details again. (A Google Account can also be set up at a later time; see pages 20-21.)

- **Google services**. This includes options for which of the Google services you want to use, including backing up your phone, using location services, and sending feedback to Google.

- **Date and time**. This can be used to set the date and time, either manually or automatically.

- **Method of screen lock**. This can be used to set a lock for the phone, using a fingerprint, PIN code, pattern or a password.

- **Screen layout**. This can be used to create a larger interface on the phone's screen, by changing the size of the items on it and the font size.

Most routers require a password when they are accessed for the first time by a new device. This is a security measure to ensure that other people cannot gain unauthorized access to your router and Wi-Fi.

The Wi-Fi has to be connected in order for a Google Account to be created or signed in to during the setting up of the phone.

Since Android is owned by Google, much of its functionality is provided through a Google Account.

Android and Google

Most phones are linked to specific companies for the provision of their services and selection of apps: Apple for the iPhone, Microsoft for the Windows Phone, and Google for phones using Android, as well as the phone's manufacturer (e.g. Samsung). As with the other phones, for Android phones you must have a linked account to get the most out of your phone. This is a Google Account, and is created free of charge with a Google email address (Gmail) and a password. Once it has been created, your Google Account will give you access to a number of the built-in Android apps and also additional services such as backing up and storing your content online.

When you first set up your phone you can enter your Google Account details, or select to create a new account. You can also do this at any time by accessing one of the apps that requires access to a Google Account. These include:

- **Play Store**, for obtaining more apps.

- **Play Movies & TV**, for obtaining movies and TV shows.

- **Play Books**, for obtaining books.

- **News** app for displaying news stories.

When you access one of these apps you will be prompted to create a Google Account. You do not have to do so at this point, but it will give you access to the full range of Google Account services.

Other apps such as the Photos app for storing and viewing photos can be used on their own, but if a Google Account has been set up, the content can be backed up automatically.

If you already have a Gmail Account, this will also serve as your Google Account, and the login details (email address and password) can be used for both.

When you buy anything through your Google Account, such as music, apps or movies, you will have to enter your credit or debit card details (unless you are downloading a free app), which will be used for future purchases through your Google Account.

Google

Sign in

Use your Google Account. Learn more

Email or phone

Forgot email?

Create account   Next

Some of the benefits of a Google Account include:

- Access from any computer or mobile device with web access, from the page **accounts.google.com/**
Once you have entered your account details you can access the online Google services, including your Calendar, Gmail and the Play Store.

- Keep your content synchronized and backed up. With a Google Account, all of your linked data will be automatically synchronized so that it is available for all web-enabled devices, and it will also be backed up by the Google servers if you have set this up in Google Drive (see page 126).

If you buy items from the Play Store through your Google Account on the web, they will also be available on your Android phone.

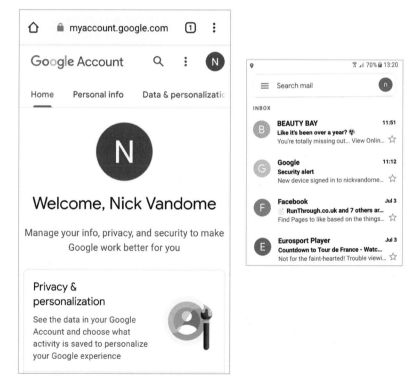

A new Google Account can also be created within **Settings** > **Cloud and accounts** > **Accounts** on your phone. Tap on the **Add account** button and tap on the **Google** button. Then enter the required details for the new Google Account (see pages 20-21).

- Peace of mind that your content is protected. There is a **Security** section on your Google Account web page where you can apply various security settings and alerts.

19

Creating a Google Account

A new Google Account can be created in the following different ways:

- During the initial setup of your Android phone.

- When you first access one of the relevant apps, as explained on page 18.

- From the **Settings** app, by selecting **Cloud and accounts** > **Accounts** > **Add account**.

For each of the above, the process for creating the Google Account is the same:

Don't forget

During the account setup process there is also a screen for account recovery, where you can add an answer to a question so that your account details can be retrieved by Google if you forget them.

20

1 If you already have an account, enter your sign-in details, or tap on the **Create account** option

Google

Sign in

Use your Google Account. Learn more

Email or phone

Forgot email?

Create account   Next

2 Enter the first and last name for the new account user, then tap on the **Next** button

Google

Create a Google Account

Enter your name

First name
Nick

Last name
Vandome

Next

3 Enter a username (this will also become your Gmail address), then tap on the **Next** button at the bottom of the screen

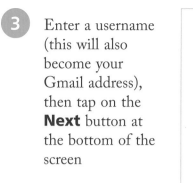

Google

Choose your Gmail address

Pick a Gmail address or create your own

○ nickvandome87@gmail.com

○ vandomenick@gmail.com

○ Create a different Gmail address

Next

A username for a Google Account is a unique name created by the user, which is suffixed by @gmail.com.

4 Create a password for the account and then re-enter it for confirmation. Tap on the **Next** button at the bottom of the screen

Google

Create a strong password

Create a strong password with a mix of letters, numbers and symbols

Create password

••••••••

At least 8 characters

Confirm

••••••••

Next

If your chosen username has already been taken, you will be prompted to amend it. This can usually be done by adding a sequence of numbers to the end of it, but make sure you remember the sequence correctly.

5 The account details are displayed. Tap on the **Next** button to sign in with your new account

Google

Thanks, Nick

Email
nickvandome87@gmail.com

Password
••••••••

Your Google Account comes with access to everything Google: apps, music, games, and more

Next

21

Using a Touchscreen

The traditional method of interacting with a computer is by using a mouse and a keyboard as the input devices. However, this has all changed with smartphones; they are much more tactile devices that are controlled by tapping and swiping on the touchscreen. This activates and controls the apps and settings on the phone, and enables you to add content with the virtual keyboard that appears at the appropriate times.

Gently does it

Touchscreens are sensitive devices and only require a light touch to activate the required command. To get the best out of your touchscreen:

- Tap, swipe or press gently on the screen. Do not use excessive force and do not keep tapping with increasing pressure if something does not work in the way in which you expected. Instead, try performing another action and then returning to the original one.

- Tap with your fingertip rather than your fingernail. This will be more effective in terms of performing the required operation, and is better for the surface of the touchscreen.

- For the majority of touchscreen tasks, tap, press or swipe at one point on the screen. The exception to this is zooming in and out on certain items (such as web pages), which can be done by swiping outwards and pinching inwards with thumb and forefinger.

- Keep your touchscreen dry, and make sure that your fingers are also clean and free of moisture.

- Use a cover to protect the screen when not in use, particularly if you are carrying your phone in a jacket pocket or a bag.

- Use a screen cloth to keep the screen clean and free of fingerprints and smears. The touchscreen should still work if it has fingerprints and marks on it, but it will become harder to see clearly what is on the screen.

Hot tip

If you are using your phone in an area where there is likely to be moisture, such as in the kitchen if you are following a recipe, cover the touchscreen in some form of light plastic wrap to protect it from any spills or splashes.

Touchscreen controls

Touchscreens can be controlled with three main types of actions. These are:

- **Tapping**. Tap once on an item such as an app to activate it. This can also be used for the main navigation control buttons at the bottom of the touchscreen, or for items such as checkboxes when applying settings for specific items.

- **Pressing**. Press and hold on an item on the Home screen to move its position or place it in the **Favorites Tray** at the bottom of the screen.

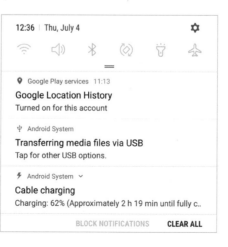

- **Swiping**. Swipe down from the top of the Home screen to access the **Notification panel** and the **Quick Settings**, and swipe left and right to view all of the available Home screens, or to scroll through photo albums.

For more information about working with apps on the Home screen and the Notification panel, see Chapter Four.

23

Using Apps

One of the great selling points for Android phones is the range of apps that are available for them. At the time of printing, there are at least 2.7 million Android apps in the Google Play Store, with others available from third-party developers. Some are free, while others are paid for.

The built-in apps are the ones that give the initial functionality to your phone, and include items such as email, web browser, calendar, calculator and maps. They appear as icons on your phone's Home screen, or in the All Apps area (see page 56), and are accessed by tapping on them once.

Managing apps

When you switch from one app to another you do not have to close down the original one that you were using. Android keeps it running in the background, but in a state of hibernation so that it is not using up any memory or processing power on your phone. To do this:

 Tap on an app to open it and move through its screens as required.

Tap on the **Home** button on the phone's Navigation bar at the bottom of the screen to return to the Home screen at any point. The app will remain open in the background

 Tap on the app again. It will open up at the point at which you left it

You can also move back to the Home screen by tapping on the **Back** button. This takes you back through the screens that you have accessed within the app, until you reach the app's Home screen, at which point the next screen back will be the phone's Home screen.

If your phone is running low on memory it will automatically close any open apps to free up more memory. The ones that have been inactive for the longest period of time are closed first.

New apps for Android phones are available through the Play Store, or directly from the developer's website. They can be downloaded from there and will then appear on your phone. (See pages 134-139.)

Play Store

2 Models of Android Phones

There are a huge number of different Android phones on the market. This chapter looks at some of the leading manufacturers and a few of the phones they make.

Don't forget

RAM stands for Random Access Memory, which is the memory that is used to process operations that the phone is performing. Usually, the more RAM, the better.

Hot tip

A large number of smartphones, particularly the high-end models, have the capacity for additional storage through the use of a microSD card, which fits into a slot on the side of the body of the phone. This can increase the phone's storage considerably.

Samsung Phones

Samsung is the market leader in terms of the number of smartphones sold globally, partly due to the fact that it offers a considerable range of models, from its flagship Galaxy S models to a range of cheaper models.

Several Samsung smartphones models use the TouchWiz interface as an overlay for Android.

Some of the Samsung phones to look at include:

Galaxy S series

This includes the Galaxy S10 and S10+, which are Samsung's latest rivals to Apple's iPhone. The specifications include:

- Display: 6.1 inches (diagonally); 6.4 inches for S10+.

- Weight: 157g; 175g for S10+.

- RAM: 8GB; 12GB for S10+.

- Memory: internal – up to 1TB, with a microSD card.

- Operating system: Android 9.0 Pie for both.

- Main camera: 12MP for both.

- Fingerprint sensor for unlocking the phone.

- Battery: non-removable Li-Ion 3400mAh; 4100mAh for S10+.

Galaxy A series

This is Samsung's mid-range series of phones, and includes the Galaxy A3, Galaxy A5 and Galaxy A7 (which have increasing screen sizes). Some of the specifications for them are (for A3, A5 and A7 respectively):

- Display: 4.7 inches, 5.2 inches, 5.7 inches (diagonally).

- Weight: 138g, 157g, 186g.

- RAM: 2GB, 3GB, 3GB.

- Memory: internal – 16GB, 32GB, 32GB.

- Operating system: Android 6.0.1 Marshmallow, for all.

- Main camera: 13MP, 16MP, 16MP.

- Fingerprint sensor for unlocking the phone, for all.

- Battery: non-removable Li-Ion 2350mAh, 3000mAh, 3600mAh.

Generally, higher-specification models of smartphones – i.e. the most powerful and expensive – come with the latest version of Android, or can upgrade to it. Other models may be limited in terms of the version of Android that they can run.

Galaxy J series

This is Samsung's range of budget smartphones, and includes the Galaxy J1, Galaxy J5 and Galaxy J7 (which have increasing screen sizes). Some of the specifications for them are (for the J1, J5 and J7 respectively):

- Display: 4.5 inches, 5.2 inches, 5.5 inches (diagonally).

- Weight: 131g, 159g, 170g.

- RAM: 1GB, 2GB, 2GB.

- Memory: internal – 8GB, 16GB, 16GB.

- Operating system: Android 5.1.1 Lollipop, Android 6.0.1 Marshmallow, Android 6.0.1 Marshmallow.

- Main camera: 5MP, 13MP, 13MP.

- Fingerprint sensor for unlocking the phone (some models).

- Battery: removable Li-Ion 2050mAh, 3100mAh, 3300mAh.

The phones listed in this chapter are just a small number of the hundreds of Android models that are on the market, covering different specifications and different versions of the Android operating system.

Google Phones

Since Android is owned by Google, it makes sense for them to have their own Android phone. This is the Google Pixel 3 phone, which is the successor to the first Pixel phone. It comes in the standard model or in the XL model.

The Pixel 3 is a high-specification smartphone and, unlike the majority of Android phones on the market, comes with the latest version of Android (9.0 Pie at the time of printing). Also, the Pixel 3 will be the first phone that can update to the next version of Android when it is released.

Android on the Google Pixel 3 is the purest form of the operating system, since – unlike other manufacturers who use Android on their phones – there is no overlay on top of the standard operating system.

The Google Pixel 3
Some of the specifications of the Google Pixel 3 are:

- Display: 5.5 inches (diagonally).

- Weight: 148g.

- RAM: 4GB.

- Memory: internal – 64/128GB.

- Operating system: Android 9.0 Pie.

- Main camera: 12.2MP.

- Fingerprint sensor (on the back of the phone) for unlocking the phone.

- Battery: non-removable Li-Po 2915mAh.

Beware

The Google Pixel 3 does not have a microSD card slot for additional memory, but has unlimited cloud storage for photos.

Sony Phones

Sony is another major player in the smartphone market, and has a reputation for producing phones with particularly high-quality cameras.

Xperia 10

The Xperia series is the main range of Sony smartphones, with the Xperia 10 being the flagship model. Some of its specifications are:

- Display: 6.0 inches (diagonally).

- Weight: 162g.

- RAM: 3/4GB.

- Memory: internal – 64GB (upgradable to 1TB using the internal microSD card slot).

- Operating system: Android 9.0 Pie.

- Main camera: 13MP.

- Fingerprint sensor for unlocking the phone.

- Battery: non-removable Li-Ion 2870mAh.

Other Sony smartphones to look at include: the Xperia XZ2, the Xperia XZ3, the Xperia L3, and the Xperia XZ1.

Motorola Phones

Motorola smartphones are produced by Motorola Mobility, a company that was spun out of the original Motorola. Motorola Mobility was acquired by Google in 2011, and it was then subsequently sold to the Chinese firm Lenovo in 2014. In 2016 Lenovo announced that the Motorola smartphones would use the Moto branding.

Moto G7

The flagship Moto smartphone is the G7, and some of its specifications include:

- Display: 6.2 inches (diagonally).

- Weight: 172g.

- RAM: 4GB.

- Memory: internal – 64GB (upgradable to 1TB using the internal microSD card slot).

- Operating system: Android 9.0 Pie.

- Main camera: 12MP.

- Fingerprint sensor for unlocking the phone.

- Battery: non-removable Li-Ion 3000mAh.

Don't forget

Other Motorola smartphones to look at include: the One Vision, the Moto E5, the Moto Z4, and the Moto G6.

HTC Phones

HTC is a Taiwanese company that was at the forefront of the development of smartphones using the Android operating system. Despite an up-and-down performance in the smartphone market, HTC has produced a successful range of phones, with one of the high-end models being the HTC 12+.

HTC 12+

The specifications for the HTC 12+ include:

- Display: 6.0 inches (diagonally).

- Weight: 157g.

- RAM: 3GB.

- Memory: internal – 32GB (upgradable to 1TB using the internal microSD card slot).

- Operating system: Android 8.0 Oreo.

- Main camera: 13MP.

- Fingerprint sensor for unlocking the phone.

- Battery: non-removable Li-Ion 2965mAh.

Don't forget

Other HTC smartphones to look at include: the Exodus and the Desire ranges.

Huawei Phones

Huawei is a major Chinese technology company that produces a wide range of communications devices including smartphones. Most Huawei phones that use Android also use the Emotion User Interface (EMUI) overlay.

nova series

The latest flagship high-end phone from Huawei is the nova 5 (with additional models, the nova 5 Pro and the nova 5i), and some of its specifications include:

- Display: 6.39 inches (diagonally).

- Weight: 171g.

- RAM: 8GB.

- Memory: internal – up to 256GB.

- Operating system: Android 9.0 Pie.

- Main camera: 48MP.

- Fingerprint sensor for unlocking the phone.

- Battery: non-removable Li-Po 3500mAh.

Don't forget

Other Huawei smartphones to look at include: the Y9 Prime, the P30, the Y7, and the Enjoy 9e.

32

Lenovo Phones

Lenovo is another large Chinese technology company that produces personal computers, laptops, tablets and smartphones, alongside a wide range of other devices.

Lenovo 6 series

The latest high-end range of Lenovo smartphones is the Z6 series. Some of the specifications of the Z6 are:

- Display: 6.39 inches (diagonally).

- Weight: 185g.

- RAM: Up to 12GB.

- Memory: internal – 512GB (upgradable to 1TB using the internal microSD card slot).

- Operating system: Android 9.0 Pie.

- Main camera: 48MP.

- Fingerprint sensor for unlocking the phone.

- Battery: non-removable Li-Po 4000mAh.

Other Lenovo smartphones to look at include: the K6 Youth and the Z5 series.

LG Phones

LG Corporation (formerly Lucky-GoldStar Corporation) is a South Korean multinational that produces a wide range of products, from washing powder and toothpaste to electronic devices. LG Corporation has produced a range of smartphones over the years, with particular success in the US.

W series

The flagship LG smartphone range is the W series, with one of the most recent models being the W30. Some of its specifications include:

- Display: 6.26 inches (diagonally).

- Weight: 172g.

- RAM: 3GB.

- Memory: internal – 32GB (upgradable to 256GB using the internal microSD card slot).

- Operating system: Android 9.0 Pie.

- Main camera: 13MP.

- Fingerprint sensor (on the back of the phone) for unlocking the phone.

- Battery: removable Li-Po 4000mAh.

Other LG smartphones to look at include: the G8 ThinQ, the V50, and the K series of budget smartphones.

3 Android Settings

As with all computers and mobile devices, Android phones have a range of settings that can be applied to specify the operation of the device and also its look and feel. This chapter looks at the range of settings that are available, and shows how to apply them to customize your Android phone exactly the way that you want it.

Accessing Settings

We all like to think of ourselves as individuals, and this extends to the appearance and operation of our electronic gadgets. An Android phone offers a range of settings so that you can set it up exactly the way that you want, and give it your own look and feel. These are available from the **Settings** app.

To access the **Settings** app on your Android phone:

The Settings app has been comprehensively updated for Android 7.0 Nougat.

Hot tip

The Settings app can be added to the Home screen, or the Favorites Tray (see page 56), by pressing and holding on it in the All Apps section and then dragging it to the required location.

Hot tip

The Settings app can also be accessed by swiping down from the top of the phone to access the Quick Settings (see page 54). From here, tap on the **Settings** button at the top of the screen.

1 Tap on the **All Apps** button (see page 56)

Apps

2 Tap on the **Settings** app

Settings

3 The full range of settings is displayed

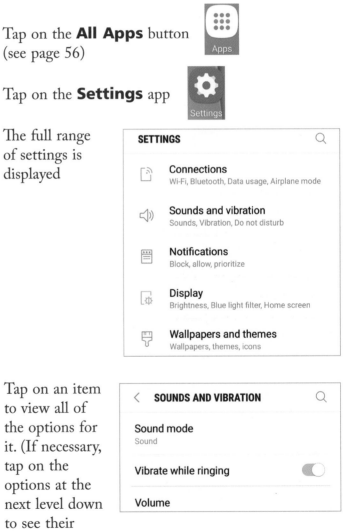

SETTINGS

Connections
Wi-Fi, Bluetooth, Data usage, Airplane mode

Sounds and vibration
Sounds, Vibration, Do not disturb

Notifications
Block, allow, prioritize

Display
Brightness, Blue light filter, Home screen

Wallpapers and themes
Wallpapers, themes, icons

4 Tap on an item to view all of the options for it. (If necessary, tap on the options at the next level down to see their own options.) Most options will have an On/Off button, a radio button or a checkbox to tap on or off

SOUNDS AND VIBRATION

Sound mode
Sound

Vibrate while ringing

Volume

Connections

These settings can include:

- **Wi-Fi**. Used for turning Wi-Fi on and off on your phone, and connecting to a router.

- **Bluetooth**. Used for connecting wirelessly to other Bluetooth-enabled devices over short distances. Both devices have to be "paired" – i.e. connected together – so that they can share content.

- **Phone visibility**. This can be used to make your phone visible to other devices, so that files can be transferred between the two.

- **Data usage**. Used to view how much data you have downloaded and which apps are using the most data.

- **Airplane mode**. Check this **On** when taking a flight, to disable any mobile communications to or from your phone.

- **NFC and payment**. This can be used to make mobile payments, using a contactless method such as Google Pay, and also connect to other compatible devices, using NFC (Near Field Communication).

- **Mobile hotspot and tethering**. This can be used to set up your phone as a mobile hotspot, so that other devices can connect to it via Wi-Fi, and then connect to the internet.

- **Location**. This can be used to view which apps have requested access to your location, or to turn on GPS.

The Wi-Fi setting can be used to connect to Wi-Fi in your own home and also to any public Wi-Fi hotspots. For both, you will usually need to use a password to access the router.

When using settings, tap on the left-facing arrowhead to return to the previous page, either within a specific setting, or to return to the main Settings Homepage.

CONNECTIONS

Wi-Fi
PLUSNET-TXJ5

Bluetooth
On

Phone visibility
Allow other devices to find your phone and transfer files.

Data usage

Airplane mode
Turn off calling, messaging functions, and Mobile data.

Hot tip

It is worth exploring the sound settings in some detail, as this is where you can turn on and off a lot of the system sounds – e.g. for when notifications and messages are received, keyboard sounds when you are typing, and for the Lock screen. There is also an option for haptic feedback (vibration feedback), which creates a small vibration when pressing certain items.

Sounds and Vibration

These settings can include:

- **Sound mode**. Use this to select from Sound, Vibrate or Mute for the phone's calls and alerts.

- **Vibrate while ringing**. Turn this **On** to enable the phone to vibrate when there is an incoming call.

- **Volume**. Use this to change the volume for a range of options, including ringtones and notifications.

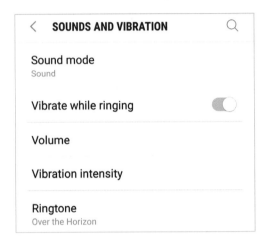

- **Vibration intensity**. Use this to specify the level of vibration for a range of options.

- **Ringtone**. Use this to select different ringtones to be used on the phone.

- **Vibration pattern**. Use this to select the type of vibration, if vibration is turned on.

- **Notification sounds**. Use this to specify sounds for incoming notifications.

- **Do not disturb**. Activate this to mute calls and alerts for specified times. Exceptions can also be set, such as calls from certain contacts.

- **System sounds**. This includes a range of options for the sounds that are used on the phone, including sounds when using the touchscreen and screen lock sounds.

- **Key-tap feedback**. This includes a range of options for selecting sounds when using the keypad.

Notifications

These settings are used to specify how notifications are dealt with on the phone – i.e. which apps can be activated for showing notifications, and how the notifications are displayed. The options for this are:

- **All apps**. If this is turned **On**, notifications can be received from all of the apps on the phone. If the All apps option is **Off**, notifications for individual apps can be turned **On** from the list below the All apps option.

If **All apps** is turned **On**, there could be a large number of notifications appearing on your phone, which could get rather overwhelming.

Tap on an app to access its notification options:

- **Allow notifications**. Drag this **On** to enable notifications for a specific app.

- **Show silently**. Drag this **On** to disable any sound or vibration when a notification is received.

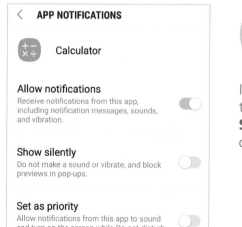

If **Show silently** is turned **On**, the **Set as priority** option is not available.

- **Set as priority**. Drag this **On** to enable an app's notification to override any Do Not Disturb settings.

Display

These settings can include:

- **Brightness**. Used to set the screen brightness, by dragging the Brightness slider.

- **Auto adjust brightness**. Used to set the screen brightness automatically, based on lighting conditions.

- **Blue light filter**. Used to reduce the amount of blue light that is emitted from the screen.

- **Screen mode**. Used to optimize the color elements of the screen to make it clearer for some users.

- **Screen zoom and font**. Used to change the size of the items on the screen and the font size used.

- **Home screen**. This can be used to change the order of the Home screens on the phone. The screens can be dragged into different positions.

- **Easy mode**. This can be used to display a simpler version of the Home screen layout.

- **Icon frames**. Used to make icons stand out more by including a frame around them.

- **LED indicator**. If this is turned **On**, the LED indicator will be displayed when the phone is charging, recording a voice message, or receiving notifications.

- **Status bar**. This can be used to show notification icons and the battery percentage at the top of the screen.

- **Screen timeout**. This can be used to specify the length of inactivity before the Lock screen appears.

- **Screen saver**. Used to display a screen saver when the screen is turned off.

- **Keep screen turned off**. This can be used to prevent the screen from being turned on accidentally.

Hot tip

Blue light can make it harder to sleep, so turn **On** the **Blue light filter** in the evening. Better still, don't use your phone during the hour before you go to bed.

Wallpapers and Themes

These settings include options for customizing three areas of the phone's appearance: wallpapers, themes and icons.

- **Wallpapers**. This can be used to change the background wallpaper for the Home screen, the Lock screen, or both. Tap on a wallpaper to view options for applying it.

Don't forget

Different brands of Android phones will have different options for the wallpaper, themes and icons.

- **Themes**. This can be used to apply a color theme for all elements on the phone.

- **Icons**. This can be used to specify how icons are displayed on the phone.

Advanced Features

These settings can include:

- **Smart stay**. This is a Samsung feature that allows for the screen to stay on while you are looking at it, regardless of the screen timeout setting.

- **Games**. This contains options for when playing games.

- **One-handed mode**. This can be used to display the keyboard at the left-hand or right-hand side of the screen, so it can be used with one hand.

- **Quick launch camera**. If this is turned **On**, the camera can be accessed by pressing the Home button twice.

- **Multi window**. This has options for displaying more than one app on the screen at a time.

- **Smart capture**. This contains additional options for capturing a screenshot of what is displayed on the screen. The options include drawing on the screenshot and cropping it.

- **Palm swipe to capture**. If this is turned **On**, you can take a screenshot by swiping your palm from right to left across the screen.

- **Direct call**. If this is turned **On**, you can call someone directly just by raising the phone to your ear, if a message from them or their contact details are displayed.

- **Smart alert**. If this is turned **On**, the phone will vibrate when picked up, if you have missed calls or messages.

- **Easy mute**. If this is turned **On**, you can mute incoming calls by putting your palm over the screen.

- **Send SOS messages**. If this is turned **On**, you can send an alert to your emergency contacts by pressing the power button three times.

- **Direct share**. This can be used to share items with contacts who are near to you with their phone.

For more information about using multi windows, see pages 67-69.

Contacts can be specified as emergency ones within the Contacts app.

42

Device Maintenance

These settings can include four main categories for keeping your Android phone in good order:

- **Battery**. This displays the health of your phone's battery and has options for optimizing the battery.

- **Storage**. This displays how much of the phone's internal storage capacity has been used, and which items are using the storage. It also has an option for freeing up storage space by deleting unnecessary items.

- **Memory**. This shows which apps are currently using the phone's memory and has an option for freeing up more memory by closing apps running in the background.

- **Device security**. This has options for scanning your phone for viruses or malware.

Use the security option to frequently scan for viruses or malware that may have infected your phone. See pages 184-185 for information on antivirus apps that can prevent viruses infecting your phone.

Apps

These settings contain information about the apps that are installed on the phone. To view the details for apps:

1 Tap on an item on the **All apps** list

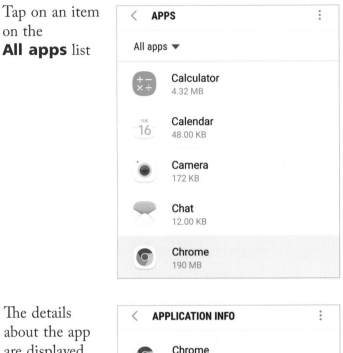

Don't forget

In some cases, the default applications will be linked to the phone's manufacturer – i.e. Samsung phones may use Samsung apps as the default for opening content such as web pages, music and videos.

2 The details about the app are displayed. Tap on the **Disable** button to prevent it from being used, or tap on the **Force Stop** button to close it

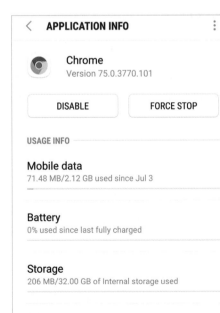

44

Lock Screen and Security

These settings can include:

- **Screen lock type**. Used to specify how the phone is unlocked once the Lock screen has been activated.

- **Info and app shortcuts**. This can be used to display certain items on the Lock screen.

- **Notifications**. This can be used to enable notifications to be shown on the Lock screen.

- **Fingerprints**. For compatible devices, this can be used to set a unique fingerprint for unlocking a phone.

- **Find my mobile**. If this is turned **On**, a linked account can be used to find a lost or stolen device, by logging on to the website associated with the account.

- **Unknown sources**. This can be used to allow apps to be installed from locations other than the Play Store.

- **Private mode**. This can be used to hide content from apps that you do not want anyone else to be able to access. An access method has to be specified when it is turned **On**, in a similar way as for the Lock screen.

- **Encrypt device**. This can be used to encrypt the data on your phone, for security purposes.

For more information about locking your phone, see pages 70-71.

For more information about using notifications, see pages 64-65.

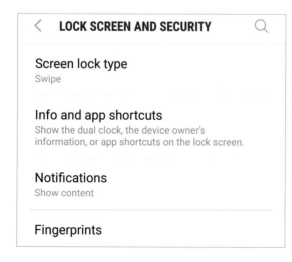

Cloud and Accounts

These settings can include:

- **Cloud**. This setting can be used to specify how items are backed up to the device's cloud service. You have to log in to the linked account to use the Cloud settings.

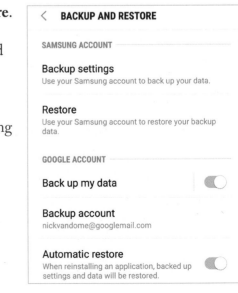

SAMSUNG ACCOUNT

Get the most from your Galaxy with your Samsung account.

Email or phone number

Password

- **Accounts**. This can be used to view existing accounts that are linked to the phone, and add new ones.

< **ACCOUNTS**   ⋮

G   Google

◻   Office

⊕   Add account

- **Backup and restore**. This can be used to specify how, and where, items are backed up on the phone and also options for restoring data from the backup.

< **BACKUP AND RESTORE**

SAMSUNG ACCOUNT

Backup settings
Use your Samsung account to back up your data.

Restore
Use your Samsung account to restore your backup data.

GOOGLE ACCOUNT

Back up my data

Backup account
nickvandome@googlemail.com

Automatic restore
When reinstalling an application, backed up settings and data will be restored.

Some Android phone manufacturers have their own cloud service for backing up and storing content from your phone. The Google Drive option can also be used with a Google Account. The Google Drive app can be downloaded from the Play Store.

46

Hot tip

Some Android phones have a separate category within the Settings app for Google settings.

General Management

These settings can include:

- **Language and input**. This can be used to specify the language used by the phone's keyboard, turn the spelling checker on or off, and specify the default virtual keyboard to be used. It can also be used to specify the use of a physical keyboard, connected to the phone.

- **Date and time**. This can be used to automatically set the date and the time for the phone, and also specify whether the 24-hour clock format is used, or not.

- **Report diagnostic info**. This can be used to send information about the phone's performance to the phone's manufacturer, via a linked account with the manufacturer. This can include diagnostic information about the phone's performance and also usage data, if permission is given for this.

> < **GENERAL MANAGEMENT**   Q
>
> LANGUAGE AND TIME
>
> Language and input
>
> Date and time
>
> SUPPORT
>
> Report diagnostic info   ⬤
>
> Marketing information
>
> Reset

- **Marketing information**. This can be used to receive special offers and recommendations from your phone's manufacturer, via a linked account.

- **Reset**. This can be used to return the phone to its original factory condition, and wipe all of the data from it. There are also options to reset specific items, such as the phone's settings.

For more information about selecting keyboards on an Android phone, see pages 100-101.

Only reset your phone to its original factory settings if you have backed up the content on it.

Accessibility

It is important for phones to be accessible to as wide a range of users as possible, including those with visual or physical and motor issues. In Android this is done through the **Accessibility** settings. To use these:

1 Tap on the **Settings** app

2 Tap on the **Accessibility** button

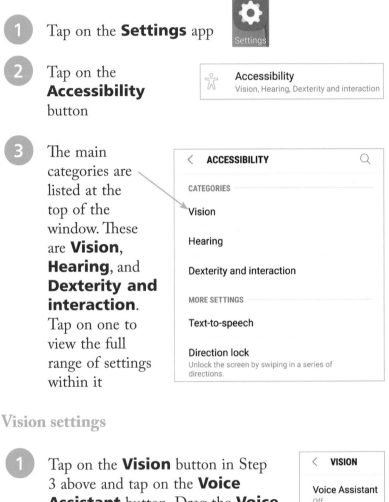

Accessibility
Vision, Hearing, Dexterity and interaction

3 The main categories are listed at the top of the window. These are **Vision**, **Hearing**, and **Dexterity and interaction**. Tap on one to view the full range of settings within it

< ACCESSIBILITY

CATEGORIES

Vision

Hearing

Dexterity and interaction

MORE SETTINGS

Text-to-speech

Direction lock
Unlock the screen by swiping in a series of directions.

Don't forget

The Vision section has a **Font size** option (accessed from the **Screen zoom and font** link) where the font size can be increased, or decreased, for compatible apps, display and system settings.

Vision settings

1 Tap on the **Vision** button in Step 3 above and tap on the **Voice Assistant** button. Drag the **Voice Assistant** button to **On**, whereby the phone will provide spoken information about items on screen and those that are being accessed

< VISION

Voice Assistant
Off

< VOICE ASSISTANT   SETTINGS

ON   ⬤

Hot tip

To turn off Voice Assistant, tap on the **Voice Assistant** button once in the second Step 1 and then double-tap on it to turn it off.

48

2 Tap on the **Settings** button at the top of the Voice Assistant window to apply options for how it functions

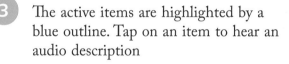

Experiment with the Accessibility settings to become familiar with the functionality of each one.

3 The active items are highlighted by a blue outline. Tap on an item to hear an audio description

SETTINGS

4 Tap on **Magnification gestures** in the Vision section to access the setting for zooming on the screen by triple-tapping on it

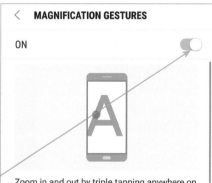

5 Drag this button **On** and triple-tap on the screen to zoom in on what is being viewed

...cont'd

Hearing settings

To use some of the Hearing settings:

 Tap on the **Hearing** option in Step 3 on page 48

in Step 3 on page 48

2 Tap on the **Flash notification** option to enable the screen to flash for notifications and calls

> **Flash notification**
> Flash the camera light when you receive notifications or when alarms sound.

3 Tap on the **Turn off all sounds** option to mute sounds for everything

> **Turn off all sounds**
> Do not play any sounds, including via the speakerphone, even if the sound mode is set to Sound.

4 Tap on the **Google subtitles CC** (Closed Captions) button

> Google subtitles (CC)

5 Drag the **Google subtitles** button to **On** to display subtitles in compatible apps – e.g. for movies or TV shows. Select the options for how the subtitles are displayed

< GOOGLE SUBTITLES (CC)

ON

Captions will look like this.

BASIC OPTIONS

Language
Default

Text size
Normal

Caption style
White on black

Beware

Only some apps support subtitles, so even if they are turned on they may not appear. Check in an app's specifications in the Play Store (see pages 134-135) to see if it supports subtitles.

see pages 134-135

50

6 Below the **Left/right sound balance** heading drag the slider to the required side to adjust the sound balance when using earphones

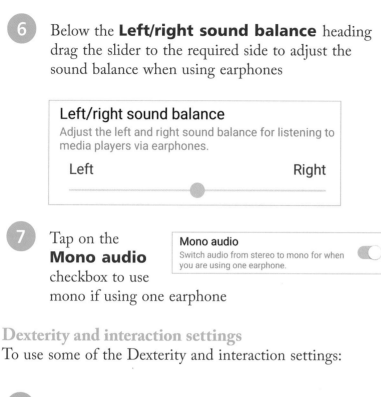

Left/right sound balance

Adjust the left and right sound balance for listening to media players via earphones.

Left   Right

7 Tap on the **Mono audio** checkbox to use mono if using one earphone

Mono audio
Switch audio from stereo to mono for when you are using one earphone.

Beware

Regardless of the sound balance, keep the overall volume on your phone to a reasonable and comfortable level; if it is too loud it may cause long-term damage, particularly when using earphones.

51

Dexterity and interaction settings

To use some of the Dexterity and interaction settings:

1 Tap on the **Dexterity and interaction** option in Step 3 on page 48

2 Tap on the **Assistant menu** option to create quick access to items

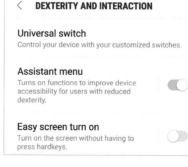

< DEXTERITY AND INTERACTION

Universal switch
Control your device with your customized switches.

Assistant menu
Turns on functions to improve device accessibility for users with reduced dexterity.

Easy screen turn on
Turn on the screen without having to press hardkeys.

3 Tap on the **Tap and hold delay** option to specify a time period before a key becomes active after pressing and holding it

Don't forget

The options in Steps 3 and 4 are located further down the Dexterity and interaction page.

4 Tap on the **Interaction control** option to specify areas of the screen that can be inactive to touch

Software Update

These settings can include:

- **Download updates manually**. This can be used to manually check to see if there are any updates for your phone waiting to be downloaded. The contents of the updates can be reviewed and the updates can then be installed, if required.

- **Download updates automatically**. If this is turned **On**, software updates will be downloaded automatically when they are available, without the need for any manual action. The download will take place when the phone is connected to a Wi-Fi network, to avoid any data charges for downloading.

- **Schedule software updates**. This can be used to specify a specific time at which software updates should be installed. It is best to select a time when the phone is not generally going to be in use, so that the updates do not interrupt any other process.

Hot tip

Keep the software on your Android phone as up-to-date as possible. This will ensure that it runs as efficiently as possible and also contains the latest security updates.

< **SOFTWARE UPDATE**   🔍

Download updates manually
Last checked on: 7/2/19
Downloading via mobile networks may result in additional charges. If possible, download via a Wi-Fi network instead.

Download updates automatically
Download software updates automatically when connected to a Wi-Fi network. You will still be able to use your device during the download.

Scheduled software updates
Your software updates will be installed at the time you set.

About Device

These settings can include:

- **My phone number**. This contains details of the phone's unique phone number.

- **Status**. This contains information about items including the phone's SIM card, its addresses for connecting to networks, and its serial number.

- **Legal information**. This contains general legal information about using the phone and the Android operating system.

⟨ **ABOUT DEVICE** 🔍
My phone number Unknown
Status View the SIM card status, device IMEI, and other information.
Legal information
Device name Galaxy S6
Model number SM-G920F
Software info View the currently installed Android version, baseband version, kernel version, build number, etc.
Battery info View your device's battery status, remaining power, and other information.

Beware

If the phone's SIM card is not installed the phone number will not be displayed under **My phone number**.

- **Device name**. This is the default name given to the phone. The name can be changed by tapping on the **Device name** heading and entering a new name.

- **Model number**. This is the unique number of the phone.

- **Software info**. This contains details about the current operating system being used by the phone, including the Android version number.

- **Battery info**. This displays information about the current status of the phone's battery, including its charging status and power level.

Quick Settings

While the full range of Android settings can be accessed from the Settings app, there is also a Quick Settings option that can be accessed from the top of the screen. To use this:

The Quick Settings have been updated for Android 7.0 Nougat.

1 Swipe down from anywhere at the top of the screen to access the **Quick Settings**

12:49 | Mon, 22 July

2 Drag down on this button to view the full range of the Quick Settings

12:49 | Mon, 22 July

Search phone and scan for nearby devices

PLUSNET-TXJ5	Mute	Bluetooth	Auto rotate
Torch	Flight mode	Power saving	Mobile data
Blue light filter	Mobile hotspot	Private mode	Location

3 Tap on this button at the top of the window and tap on the **Edit** button to amend the items in the Quick Settings

Edit

4 Drag items between the two panels to include or exclude them in the Quick Settings. The top panel contains the items that appear in the Quick Settings

| Blue light filter | Mobile hotspot | Location | Smart View |

Drag the quick setting buttons to the area above to add them to the quick settings panel.

Private mode   NFC

4 Around an Android Phone

This chapter details the Android interface and shows how to find your way around the Home screen, add apps and widgets, change the background, and lock your phone. It also covers the sophisticated range of search options that are available, including the digital voice assistant, Google Assistant, which can respond to a wide range of spoken queries.

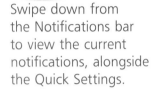

Viewing the Home Screen

Once you have set up your phone, the first screen that you see will be the Home screen. This is also where you will return to when you tap the Home button (see next page). The elements of the Home screen include:

Swipe down from the Notifications bar to view the current notifications, alongside the Quick Settings.

Notifications bar   Google Search box

Home screen area. This is where the majority of your commonly used apps and widgets will be located

12:38
Wed, July 17

G   Say "Hey Google"

Calculator   Chrome   Camera   Play Store

Maps   Gmail   Settings   Play Music

Phone   Contacts   Messages   Internet   Apps

Favorites Tray   All Apps button

On different models of Android phones, the All Apps button may be located in a slightly different position. The appearance of the Home screen may also be slightly different, depending on which apps the manufacturer has chosen to appear on the Home screen and the type of overlay used.

Navigating Around

At the bottom of the Home screen there are three buttons that can be used to navigate around your phone. On some phones these are on the screen, and on others they are on the body of the phone itself.

The Navigation buttons are:

Back. Tap on this button to go back to the most recently visited page or screen.

Home. Tap on this button to go back to the most recently viewed Home screen at any point.

Recent items. Tap on this to view the apps that you have used most recently. Tap on one of the apps to access it again. Swipe an app to the right to close the app, or tap on the cross in the top right-hand corner of the app.

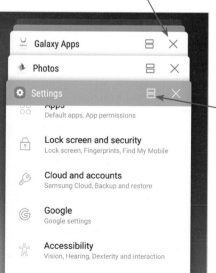

Most Android phones have several Home screens. Swipe left and right to move between them.

When the keyboard is being used, the **Back** button can also be used to hide the keyboard.

Tap on this button in the **Recent items** window to minimize a window to the top half of the screen. For more details about using multiple windows, see pages 67-69.

57

Adding Apps

The Home screen is where you can add and manage your apps. To do this:

There are thousands more apps available for download from the Play Store. Tap on this button on the Home screen to access the Play Store (see pages 134-139).

Play Store

Apps can be removed from a Home screen by pressing and holding on them, and then dragging them to the top of the screen, where a **Remove shortcut** button will appear. Drag the app over the **Remove shortcut** button. This only removes it from the Home screen, not your phone. It will still be available from the All Apps section.

1 Tap on the **All Apps** button
Apps

2 All of the built-in apps are displayed. Tap on an app to open it

3 To add an app to the Home screen, press and hold on it

4 Drag it onto the Home screen on which you want it to appear, and release it

5 The app is added to the Home screen

6 Swipe left and right to move between the available Home screens

Moving Apps

Once apps have been added to the Home screen they can be repositioned and moved to other Home screens. To do this:

1 Press and hold on an app to move it. Drag it into its new position. A light outline appears, indicating where the app will be positioned

Apps can be moved to the left or right onto new Home screens, if they are available on either side.

2 Release the app to drop it into its new position

3 To move an app between Home screens, drag it to the edge of the Home screen

Make sure that the app is fully at the edge of the Home screen, otherwise it will not move to the next one. A thin, light border should appear just before it moves to the next Home screen.

4 As the app reaches the edge of the Home screen it will automatically move to the next one. Add it to the new Home screen in the same way as in Step 2

Working with Favorites

The Favorites Tray at the bottom of the Home screen can be used to access the apps you use most frequently. This appears on all of the Home screens. Apps can be added to or removed from the Favorites Tray, as required.

Don't forget

For some phones, the Favorites Tray appears along the bottom of the screen in landscape mode; for others, it appears down the right-hand side of the screen.

Hot tip

Apps can appear in the **Favorites Tray** and also on individual Home screens, but they have to be added there each time from within the **All Apps** section.

1 The apps in the **Favorites Tray** are visible at the bottom of the screen on all Home screens

2 Press and hold on an app in the **Favorites Tray** and drag it onto the Home screen to remove it from the Favorites Tray

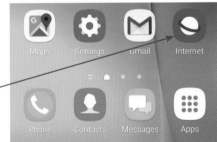

3 Press and hold on an app on the Home screen, and drag it onto a space in the **Favorites Tray** to add it there

4 The **Favorites Tray** has a limit to the number of apps that it can contain (usually four, plus the All Apps button), and if you try to add more than this, the app will spring back to its original location

Adding Widgets

Android widgets are similar to apps, except that they generally display specific content or real-time information. For instance, a photo gallery widget can be used to display photos directly on a Home screen, or a traffic widget can display updated information about traveling conditions. Widgets can be added from any Home screen:

From the panel in Step 1 you can also access Wallpapers (see page 62).

 Press and hold on an empty area on any Home screen and tap on the **Widgets** button

 Swipe up and down, or sometimes left and right, to view all of the available widgets

Widget icons on the Home screens usually appear larger than those for standard apps.

Press and hold on a widget and drop it onto a Home screen as required, in the same way as for adding apps

Changing the Background

The background (wallpaper) for all of the Home screens on your phone can be changed within the **Settings** app (**Settings** > **Wallpaper**). However, it can also be changed directly from any Home screen. To do this:

Wallpaper apps can be downloaded from the Play Store, to add a wider range of backgrounds to your phone. Enter "**wallpaper**" into the Search box of the **Apps** section of the Play Store.

1 Press and hold on an empty area on any Home screen and tap on the **Wallpapers and themes** button

2 Tap on one of the options from where you would like to select the background wallpaper and tap on a background

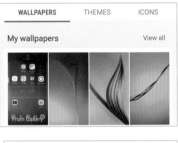

3 Select whether the background is for the **Home screen**, the **Lock screen**, or both

4 Tap on the **Set As Wallpaper** button

SET AS WALLPAPER

5 The selected background is applied to the screens selected in Step 3

Creating Folders

As you start to use your Android phone for more activities, you will probably acquire more and more apps. These will generally be for a range of tasks covering areas such as productivity, communications, music, photos, and so on. Initially it may be easy to manage and access these apps, but as the number of them increases, it may become harder to keep track of them all.

One way in which you can manage your apps is to create folders for apps covering similar subjects – e.g. one for productivity apps, one for entertainment apps; etc. To create folders for different apps:

To remove an app from a folder, press and hold on it and drag it out of the folder onto a Home screen.

 1 Drag one app over another

 2 A folder is created, and the app is added to the folder. Tap here to give the folder a name

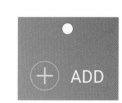

 3 Enter the name, and tap on the **Add** button to add more items to the folder

Adding folders to the Favorites Tray is a good way to make a larger number of apps available here, rather than the standard four permitted.

 4 Tap on the required items to select them for adding to the folder

63

Settings for the Notification panel can be applied in **Settings** > **Notifications**. These can be used to specify what is shown when the phone is locked and to select notifications for specific apps (see page 39).

64

Don't forget

Tap on the **Clear** button to clear all of the current notifications. If you clear the notifications it does not delete the items; they remain within their relevant apps and can be viewed there.

Using Notifications

Android phones have numerous ways of keeping you informed, from new emails and calendar events to the latest information about apps that have been downloaded and installed. To make it easier to view these items, they are grouped together in the Notification panel. This appears on the Lock screen and can also be accessed from any Home screen by swiping down from the Notifications bar.

 By default, some notifications are shown on the Lock screen. Tap on a notification here to access it directly (you must unlock your phone first – see pages 70-71)

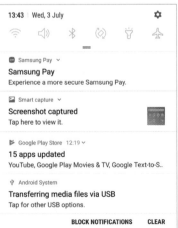

2 On any Home screen or the All Apps screen, notifications are indicated on the Notifications bar

3 Swipe down from the top of any screen to access your notifications. Some of these may display more details than on the Lock screen

 Tap on a notification to view its full details within the relevant app – e.g. a Gmail notification will open Gmail to view new emails

Settings for notifications

To specify which apps can display notifications and how they operate:

1 Within the **Settings** app, tap on the **Notifications** button

	Notifications
	Block, allow, prioritise

Notifications from apps are grouped together, so that you can view similar notifications at the same point in the Notification panel. This is a new feature in Android 7.0 Nougat.

2 Tap **Off** the **All apps** button and tap **On** individual apps to allow notifications from them

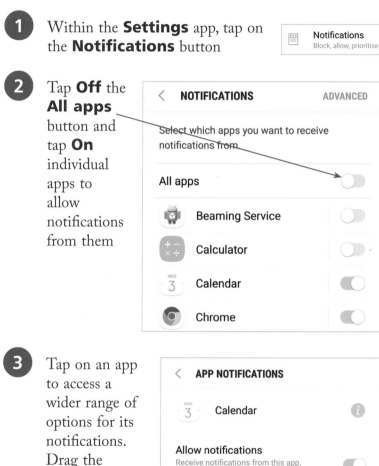

Notifications can have quick settings applied to them by pressing and holding on a notification and then tapping on one of the options in the App Notifications window. This is a new feature in Android 7.0 Nougat.

3 Tap on an app to access a wider range of options for its notifications. Drag the **Allow notifications** button to **On** to enable notifications to be displayed for the selected app

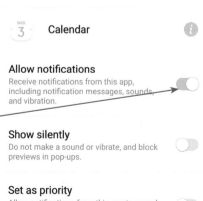

Tap on the **Show silently** option in Step 3 to mute your phone for all calls and notifications, apart from any exceptions that you specify.

Screen Rotation

By default, the content on a phone's screen rotates as you rotate the device. This means that the content can be viewed in portrait or landscape mode, depending on what is being used – e.g. for movies it may be preferable to have it in landscape mode, while for reading it may be better in portrait mode:

Screen rotation is achieved by a gyroscope sensor in the phone.

It is also possible to lock the screen so that it does not rotate when you move it. This can be useful if you are using it for a specific task and do not want to be distracted by the screen rotating if you move your hand slightly. To lock and unlock the screen rotation:

The **Auto rotate** button is sometimes called **Screen rotation** on other Android models.

1 Drag down from the top of the screen to access the **Quick Settings**

2 Tap on the **Auto rotate** button to enable screen rotation

Auto rotate

3 Tap on the **Auto rotate** button again so it displays as **Portrait**. This will lock the screen in this mode

Portrait

Using Multiple Windows

Two useful features on some Android phones (usually running Nougat 7.0 or later) is the ability to minimize one app and use others while it remains on screen (pop-up view) and also split the screen so two elements of content can be used in each part of the screen. Both of these options are located in the Multi window section of the Settings app:

The Multi window options have been updated in Android 7.0 Nougat.

1 Open the **Settings** app and tap on the **Advanced features** option

> ⚙ **Advanced features**
> Games, One-handed mode

2 Tap on the **Multi window** option

> **Multi window**
> Show more than one app at the same time.

3 Drag the **Pop-up view gesture** and **Split screen view action** buttons to **On** to enable both of these. An example of both is shown in the panel at the top of the Multi window screen

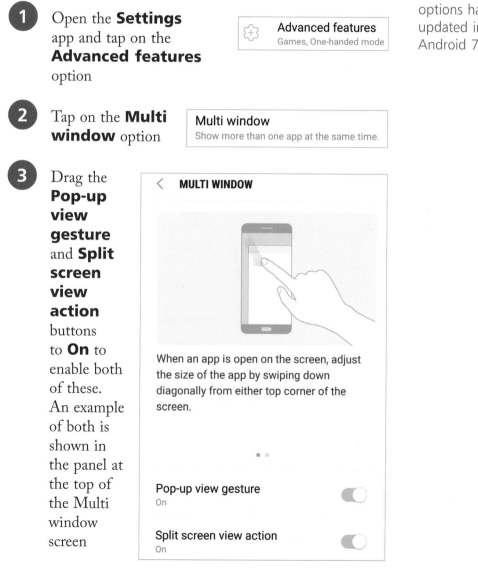

...cont'd

Pop-up view

This view can be used to display one minimized window, while other apps can still be used. To do this:

Pop-up view is a new feature introduced with Android phones using Android 7.0 Nougat.

1 Open an app and press and hold on its top-left, or top-right, corner

2 Drag the corner of the app diagonally to resize it. Other apps will appear behind it once it has been resized

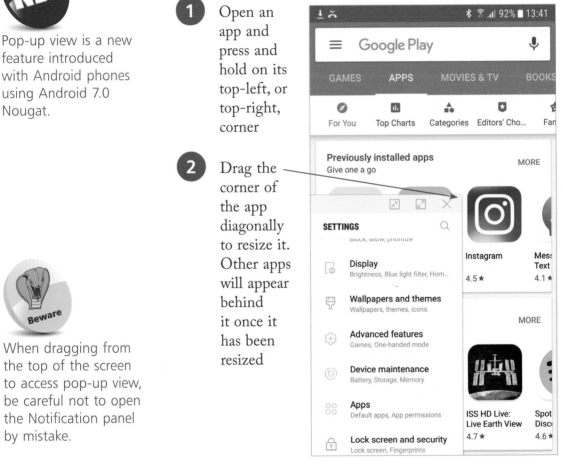

Beware

When dragging from the top of the screen to access pop-up view, be careful not to open the Notification panel by mistake.

3 For the pop-up app, tap on these buttons to, from left to right: minimize the app to a thumbnail icon on the Home screen; return the app to full-screen mode; or close the app

Split screen view

This view can be used to split the screen horizontally to enable different content to be displayed and accessed in each section. To do this:

Split screen view is a new feature introduced with Android phones using Android 7.0 Nougat.

1 Open an app and press and hold on the **Recent items** button

2 The currently active app is shown at the top of the screen. The Recent items panel is displayed at the bottom of the screen, with the other currently open apps

3 Drag on the middle bar to resize the two panels

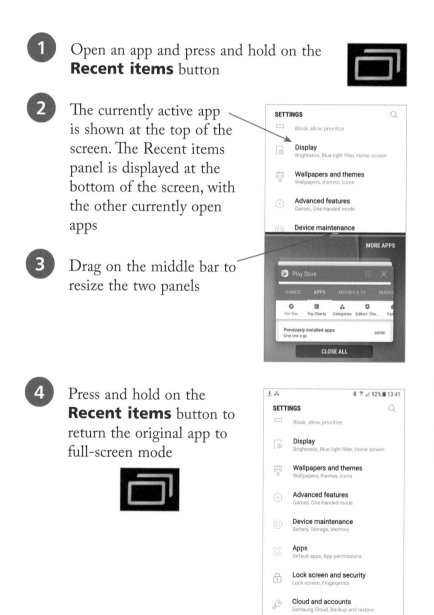

4 Press and hold on the **Recent items** button to return the original app to full-screen mode

In split screen view, the content in each panel can be used independently from the other, while they are both displayed.

Locking Your Phone

Security is an important issue for any computing device, and this applies to physical security as much as online security. For Android phones it is possible to place a digital lock on the screen so that only someone who knows the details of the lock can open it. There are different ways in which a lock can be set.

1 Tap on the **Settings** app

2 Tap on the **Lock screen and security** button

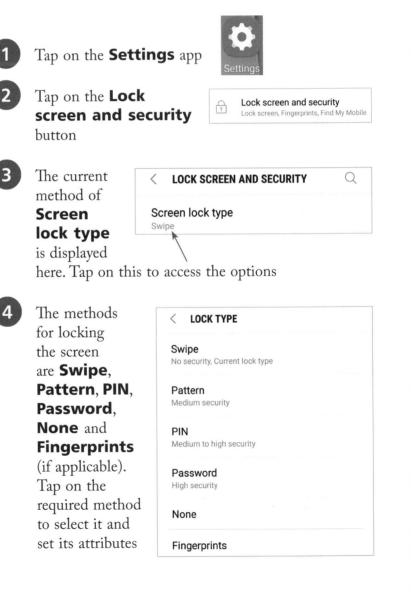

🔒 **Lock screen and security**
Lock screen, Fingerprints, Find My Mobile

3 The current method of **Screen lock type** is displayed here. Tap on this to access the options

< **LOCK SCREEN AND SECURITY** 🔍

Screen lock type
Swipe

4 The methods for locking the screen are **Swipe**, **Pattern**, **PIN**, **Password**, **None** and **Fingerprints** (if applicable). Tap on the required method to select it and set its attributes

< **LOCK TYPE**

Swipe
No security, Current lock type

Pattern
Medium security

PIN
Medium to high security

Password
High security

None

Fingerprints

Beware

The Swipe option is the least secure and is only really useful for avoiding items being activated accidentally when your phone is not in use; it is not a valid security method. The most secure method is a password containing letters, numbers and symbols, or fingerprints.

5 For the **PIN** (or **Password**) option, enter your chosen PIN in the box and tap on the **Continue** button. Enter the PIN again for confirmation. This will then need to be entered whenever you want to unlock the phone

SET PIN

PIN must contain at least 4 digits.

•••|

Remember this PIN. It will be required after you restart your phone.

CANCEL

1	2 ABC	3 DEF
4 GHI	5 JKL	6 MNO
7 PQRS	8 TUV	9 WXYZ
⌫	0 +	Done

Hot tip

PIN stands for Personal Identification Number, and is a sequence of numbers chosen by and known only to you.

6 For the **Pattern** option, drag over the keypad to create the desired pattern, repeat to confirm, and then this will be enabled on your Lock screen

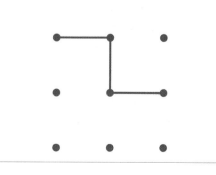

SET PATTERN

Release finger when finished.

Remember this Pattern. It will be required after you restart your phone.

Hot tip

Whenever your phone goes to sleep it will need to be unlocked before you can use it again. Sleep mode can be activated by pressing the **On/Off** button once. After a period of inactivity it will go into Sleep mode automatically: the length of time until this happens can be specified within **Settings** > **Display** > **Screen timeout**.

71

Searching

Since Android is owned by Google, it is unsurprising that phones with this operating system come with the power of Google's search functionality. Items can be searched for within the phone itself, or you can perform searches on the web. This can be done by typing in the Google Search box and also by using the voice search option. To search for items on an Android phone:

 The Google Search box is usually found on the Home screen, or it can be accessed through the Google app, or added via a widget (see page 61)

 Begin typing a word or phrase. As you type, corresponding suggestions will appear, both for on the web and for apps on the phone (if applicable)

G	ineasysteps	✕
🔍	ineasysteps	↖
🔍	ineasysteps **download**	↖
🔍	ineasysteps **ebooks**	↖
🔍	ineasysteps **python**	↖

 As you continue to type, the suggestions will become more defined

Don't forget

On some phones, the search option is indicated by a magnifying glass with the word Google next to it.

4 Tap on an app result to open it directly on your phone, or tap on this button on the keyboard to view the results from the web

Voice search

To use the voice search functionality on your phone, instead of typing a search query:

The voice search functionality can also be used for items such as finding directions, setting alarms and finding photos on your phone.

1 Tap on the microphone button in the Search box

2 When the colored dots appear, speak the word or phrase for which you want to search

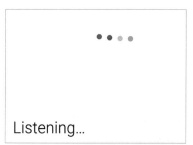

Listening...

...cont'd

 3 You can use voice search to find or open items on your phone or from the web. On your phone you can use voice search to open apps, such as your Gmail app

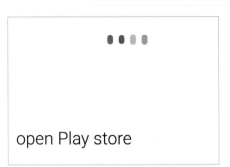

open Play store

4 The app opens in the same way as if you had tapped on it from the Home screen

The phrase displayed in the voice search window is sometimes a summary of what you actually say. For instance, if you say, **"Please open Gmail app"**, the words **"open gmail"** may be displayed.

5 If you search for items on the web, Google will use your location (if enabled) and also your search history to give you more accurate results. For instance, if you search for "Indian restaurants" it will display the results for those closest to your location

Google Assistant

One innovation from Google on some Android phones is the Google Assistant. This is a personal digital assistant that responds to voice commands. To use the Google Assistant:

1 Press and hold on the **Home** button to start setting up Google Assistant

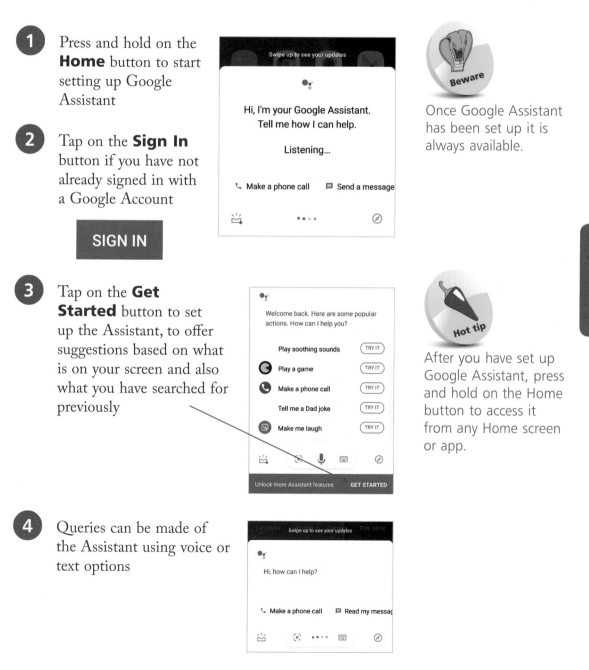

2 Tap on the **Sign In** button if you have not already signed in with a Google Account

SIGN IN

3 Tap on the **Get Started** button to set up the Assistant, to offer suggestions based on what is on your screen and also what you have searched for previously

4 Queries can be made of the Assistant using voice or text options

Beware

Once Google Assistant has been set up it is always available.

Hot tip

After you have set up Google Assistant, press and hold on the Home button to access it from any Home screen or app.

...cont'd

5 Speak the query, such as "find nearest coffee shop"

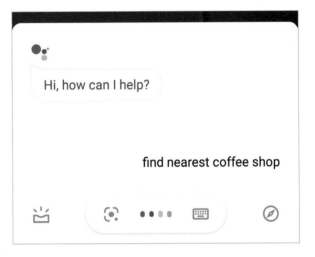

Hot tip

Google Assistant is an excellent option for finding locations when you are traveling. However, this requires a Wi-Fi or cellular network connection, with 3G, 4G or 5G.

Don't forget

Location must be checked **On** (**Settings** > **Connections** > **Location**) for these services to work.

6 The Assistant displays the results. There are also options for searching for the results over the web and viewing them on a map, if applicable

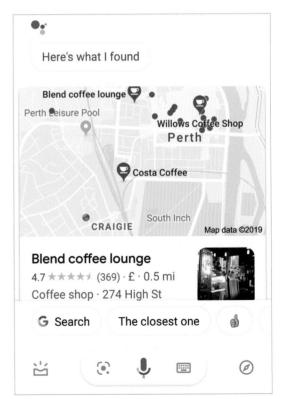

Hey Google

The Google Assistant also incorporates the "Hey Google" functionality, whereby you can use voice search commands from any screen. To set up Hey Google:

1 Once the Assistant has been set up, say "Hey Google"

2 Tap on the **I Agree** button

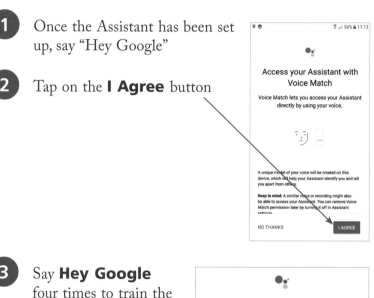

Access your Assistant with Voice Match

Voice Match lets you access your Assistant directly by using your voice.

A unique model of your voice will be created on this device, which will help your Assistant identify you and tell you apart from others.

Keep in mind: A similar voice or recording might also be able to access your Assistant. You can remove Voice Match permission later by turning it off in Assistant settings

NO THANKS   I AGREE

Don't forget

The Google Assistant can be used without training it to use your voice first. However, for Hey Google these steps have to be followed to set it up.

77

3 Say **Hey Google** four times to train the Assistant. Once this is completed, Hey Google is set up

Teach your Assistant to recognise your voice

✓ Complete

✓ Complete

⌒ Now say 'Hey Google'

Beware

4 Say **Hey Google** from any screen to access the Assistant and give it a command or a query

It may take Hey Google longer to recognize regional accents, but it should identify them after a bit of practice.

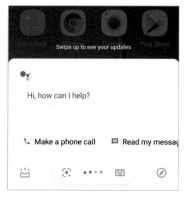

Swipe up to see your updates

Hi, how can I help?

📞 Make a phone call   📨 Read my messag

Using Google Discover

We live in an age where we want the availability of as much up-to-date information as possible. On an Android phone, one option for this is Google Discover. This is a digital assistant service that provides items such as the latest traffic information for your area, flight information or the results from your favorite sports team. The information displayed is tailored to your needs according to your location and the type of content that you access.

When Google Discover is activated this also turns on your location history so that Google can make use of the location data that is collected by your phone, once you have authorized it to do so.

Google Discover cards

The functionality of Google Discover is provided by cards. These display up-to-date information for a variety of topics. You can apply your own specific settings for each card, and these will then display new information as it occurs. Cards appear when it is deemed that they are necessary, based on your location. So, if you are traveling in a different country, you will see a different range of cards from those when you are at home. Some of the most popular default cards include those for traveling to specific destinations (such as work) and sports cards.

To use Google Discover on your phone you have to be connected to the internet via Wi-Fi or cellular.

The Google Discover page can be accessed from the Google app in Step 1 on the next page.

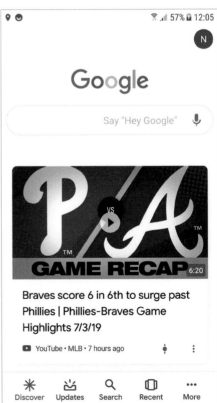

Accessing Google Discover

By default, Google Discover is not on (although it can be turned on during the initial setup process for your phone). To activate it so that it works for you in the background:

1 Tap on the **Google** app

2 Tap on the **Turn On** button at the bottom of the screen

3 Select an existing account for using Google Discover, or tap on the **Add an Account** option to add a different account to use

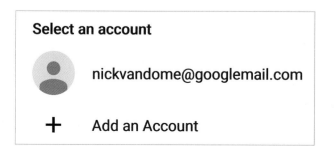

Google Discover also accesses your web history, in order to provide you with as much relevant information as possible. This is stored as part of your Google Account and can be accessed by logging in with your account details at the website **accounts.google.com** and accessing the **My Activity** section.

Some of the Google Discover cards include: weather, traffic, sports, public transport, next appointment, news updates, and travel.

The Google Search box is located at the top of the Google Discover Home screen. This can be used to search your Google Discover cards, your phone and also the web.

To delete a card, swipe it left or right off the screen. The card will come back the next time that the item is updated. To remove a card completely, click the **Never show...** option in Step 3.

...cont'd

Around Google Discover

When you first activate Google Discover you will see the Home screen. This is where your cards will show up, and from where you can access all of the settings for individual cards, such as selecting the way in which weather updates are displayed.

1 Active cards are shown on the Home screen

2 Tap here to view the card's individual settings

3 Specific settings can be applied for individual cards, such as the way in which the Weather card displays its information

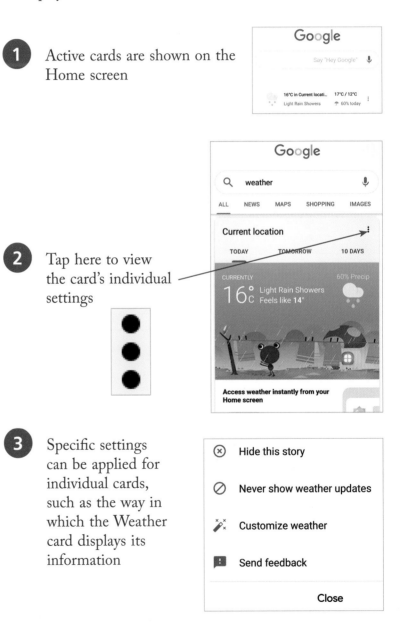

Customizing Google Discover

Google Discover can be customized so that you get exactly the type of information that you want. To do this:

1 Tap on the **More** button at the bottom of the Google Discover window

2 Tap on the **Customize Discover** button

≡ **Customize Discover**

3 Google Discover makes suggestions on items to follow, based on what you have previously looked at, and your web browsing history. Drag this button **On** to enable a specific type of update to be used

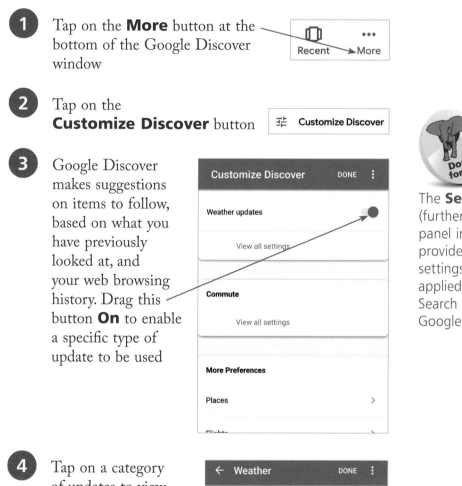

4 Tap on a category of updates to view the options for customizing it

The **Settings** option (further down the panel in Step 2) provides a range of settings that can be applied for Google Search and also Google Assistant.

...cont'd

5 Swipe down to view more options for adding categories for the Google Discovery feed

More Preferences

Places   >

Flights   >

Parking   >

∨   Show more

6 Within some categories, there are suggestions for items to be included in Google Discovery. Tap on this button next to a suggestion to add it

← Sports   DONE   ⋮

Notifications for Sports

Teams you follow

Atlanta Braves   ×

Atlanta Hawks   ×

Leagues you follow

Based on activity

Topics that may appear in Discover based on your past activity.

Boston Red Sox   ⊘   ⊕

7 Updates on items that have been added appear on the Homepage of the Google Discovery feed

Google

Say "Hey Google" 🎤

17°C in Current locati...   18°C / 11°C
Rain   ☂ 70% today

GAME RECAP   5:45

5 Calls and Contacts

This chapter focuses on using an Android phone to make and receive calls, and also how to add the details of people who have contacted you.

Adding Contacts

Given the range of uses to which you can put your Android phone, it is sometimes overlooked that one of its original functions is to make phone calls to people. This can be done by typing a number directly into the phone dialer (see page 92). However, it is generally better to first add contacts to your phone and then you can use these details to keep in touch with them in a variety of ways. To add a contact:

The Contacts option can also be accessed from the **Phone** app.

1 Tap on the **Contacts** app

Contacts

2 By default, the Contacts app will only show the details of the SIM card currently installed. Tap on the **+** button to add a new contact to your Contacts list

3 Select where you want to store the contact. Generally, it is better to store Contacts on the **SIM card**, rather than **Phone**, so if you get a new phone you can move all of your contacts by simply transferring the SIM card

If you have a Google Account, contacts can be added here too so that they are available from the Contacts app and the Phone app.

Save contact to

Phone

SIM card

Google
nickvandome@googlemail.com

4 Enter the details for the new contact and tap on the **Save** button. (Tap here to change where the contact details are stored)

Hot tip

If you save a contact to the SIM card, it will be available if you put the SIM card into another phone.

5 The new contact is added to the Contacts app (which is also accessed from the **Contacts** tab in the **Phone** app)

6 Tap on a contact to see their details. Tap on the speech bubble icon to create a text message for the selected contact, the phone icon to make a call to them, or the video icon to make a video call

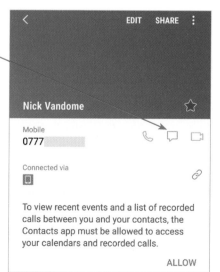

Saving Contacts from Calls

Another quick way to add a contact is to ask someone to phone you so that you can then copy their number directly from your phone to your Contacts. You do not even have to answer the phone to do this.

When you receive a call while you are using another app, accept it by tapping the green **Answer** button and to reject a call, tap the red **Decline** button.

 Once someone has phoned, tap on the **Phone** button

2 Tap on the **Recents** tab. The call or text will be displayed. Tap on the number and tap on the **Details** button

3 Tap on the **Create Contact** option

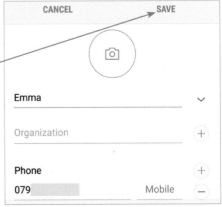

The **Recents** page shows the most recent calls and texts that you have received.

4 Enter details for the contact and tap on the **Save** button at the top of the screen

SAVE

Saving Contacts from Texts

Contacts can also be saved from text messages:

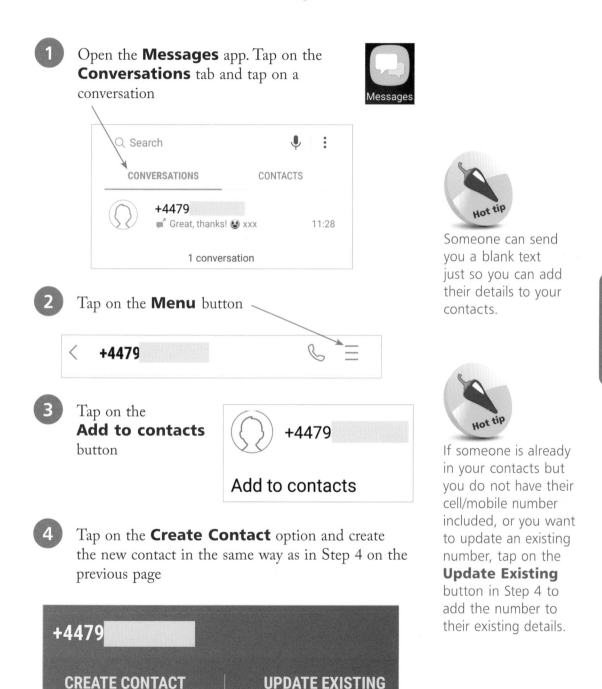

1 Open the **Messages** app. Tap on the **Conversations** tab and tap on a conversation

2 Tap on the **Menu** button

3 Tap on the **Add to contacts** button

4 Tap on the **Create Contact** option and create the new contact in the same way as in Step 4 on the previous page

Hot tip

Someone can send you a blank text just so you can add their details to your contacts.

Hot tip

If someone is already in your contacts but you do not have their cell/mobile number included, or you want to update an existing number, tap on the **Update Existing** button in Step 4 to add the number to their existing details.

Managing Contacts

Sometimes you may end up with contacts on your phone (if you have selected to save them onto your **Device** rather than **SIM**) and you will want to transfer them to your SIM card. This is useful if you are going to transfer your SIM card to another phone. To do this:

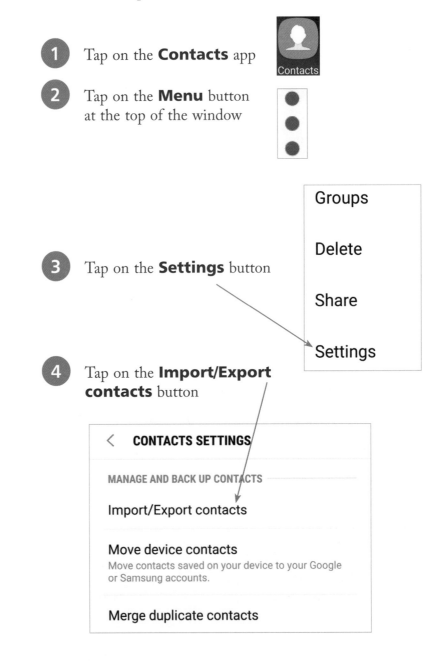

1 Tap on the **Contacts** app

Contacts

2 Tap on the **Menu** button at the top of the window

Groups

Delete

Share

3 Tap on the **Settings** button

Settings

4 Tap on the **Import/Export contacts** button

<   **CONTACTS SETTINGS**

MANAGE AND BACK UP CONTACTS

Import/Export contacts

Move device contacts
Move contacts saved on your device to your Google or Samsung accounts.

Merge duplicate contacts

5 Tap on the **Import** or **Export** buttons to start the transfer of contacts

< IMPORT/EXPORT CONTACTS

IMPORT CONTACTS

Import vCard files (VCF) from your device storage.

| IMPORT |

EXPORT CONTACTS

Export contacts to other storage locations as vCard files (VCF).

| EXPORT |

6 Select the destination for exporting contacts (or source for importing them)

Export contacts to

Device storage

SIM card

7 Since more information can be stored for a device contact than for a SIM one, some details you may have entered may be lost when moving the contact to the SIM. A dialog box appears, asking if you want to continue. If you do, tap on the **OK** button

Export to SIM card

The information in the name, phone number, and email text fields will be copied. Some contact information may be lost.

OK

One of the options for managing contacts is moving them to your Google Account, where they will be stored online in the Google cloud.

Move device contacts

Google
nickvandome@googlemail.com

Don't forget

8 Once the operation has been completed, this is shown within the Notification panel

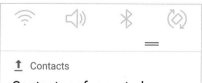

⬆ Contacts

Contacts.vcf exported.

Editing Contacts

Once contacts have been added to your Android phone you can still edit their details, whether they have been added to the phone or the SIM card, although a wider range of information can be added to a contact on the phone.

 Tap on the **Contacts** app

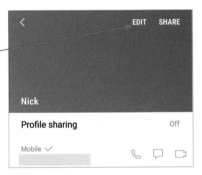

 Access a contact and tap on their name to view their details

 The current details are displayed. Tap on the **Edit** button

EDIT

90

If you have downloaded messaging apps, such as WhatsApp, the information from your Contacts list will be synced with this and any of your contacts who are using the service will automatically be displayed in the messaging app, if you agree to this when you install the WhatsApp app.

 Edit the details as required. Contacts that have been added to the phone's storage have a greater range of fields for information. If the contact has only been added to the SIM card, the only fields available will be for name and phone number

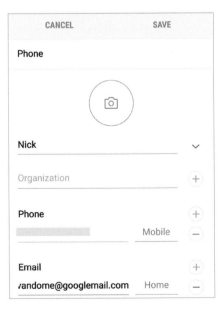

5 Tap on an item to view its options

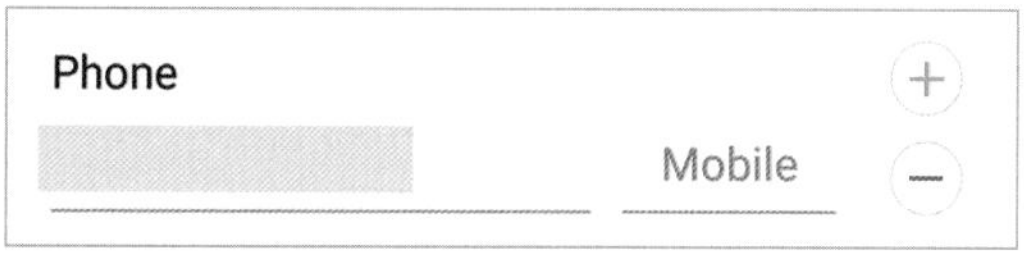

Phone		⊕
▓▓▓▓▓▓▓▓	Mobile	⊖

6 Select the options as required

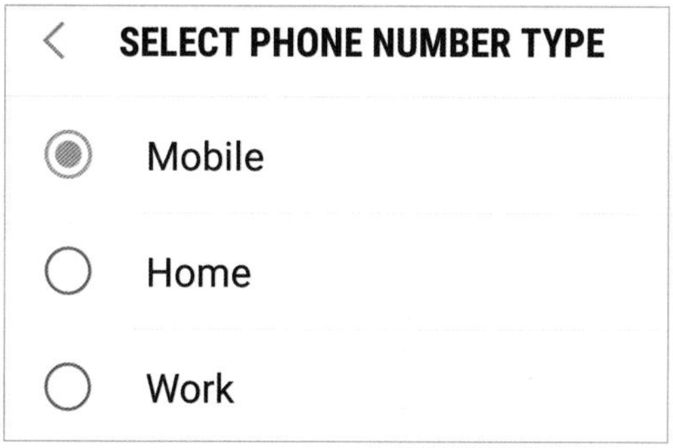

> **〈 SELECT PHONE NUMBER TYPE**
>
> ◉ Mobile
>
> ◯ Home
>
> ◯ Work

7 Tap on the **Save** button to save the editing changes

SAVE

8 Tap on the green **+** button next to an item to add an additional field for it – i.e. if you want to add more than one phone number for a contact

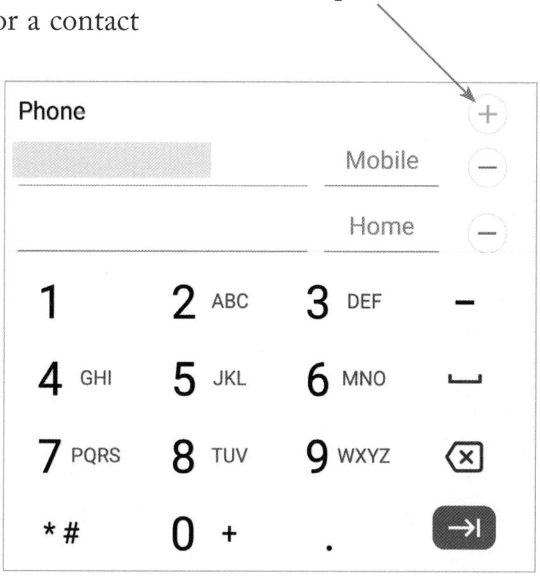

(+)

Phone		⊕
▓▓▓▓▓▓▓	Mobile	⊖
	Home	⊖

1	2 ABC	3 DEF	–
4 GHI	5 JKL	6 MNO	␣
7 PQRS	8 TUV	9 WXYZ	⌫
* #	0 +	.	→|

Making a Call

Once you have added contacts to your phone there are a number of ways in which you can phone them.

Typing a number

You can make a call by accessing the phone dialer and typing a contact's number on the keypad. To do this:

You can also create shortcuts to speed dial specific contacts, by pressing and holding a digit on the keypad and clicking **OK**, then selecting the contact from your Contacts list. Once set up, you can then just press and hold that digit to dial that particular number.

Tap on this button in Step 4 to make a video call to someone with a compatible device (i.e. another Android phone that supports video calls), instead of a voice call.

1 Tap on the **Phone** app

2 Tap on the **Keypad** button at the bottom of the screen. Type the person's number on the keypad. As the number is entered, corresponding names will be displayed from your Contacts list

3 Tap on the contact's name to display their full number

4 Tap on the **Call** button to call the number

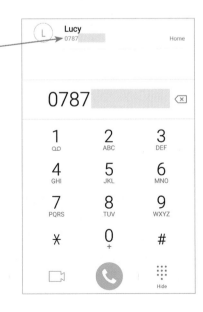

Searching for a contact

Once you have added contacts to your Contacts list you can access them and then call them. To do this:

1 Tap on the **Phone** app

2 Tap on the **Contacts** tab. At the top of the Contacts list is a Search box

3 Tap in the Search box and type a name you want to find

4 All matching results are shown. The more characters of a name that you type, the more the search results will be narrowed down. Tap on the contact you want to call

Making a quick call

It is also possible to place a call to a contact in your Contacts list, just using one swipe. To do this:

1 Access the Contacts list

2 Swipe to the right on the contact's name. The green **Call** button appears and the call is connected automatically

Hot tip

Swipe to the left on a contact's name to send them a text message, rather than make a call.

Receiving a Call

When you receive a call, the caller's name will show up on the screen (if they are in your contacts), accompanied by a ringtone (see pages 97-98).

Hot tip

On some Android models, if the caller has sent you any text messages, the latest one will be displayed on the **Incoming call** screen.

Hot tip

Tap on the **Send Message** button in Step 2 to reject the call but send the caller a text message instead.

SEND MESSAGE

1 When a call is received, the caller's name is displayed (if they have been added as a contact) along with their phone number. If their photo has been added to their contact details, this will be displayed too

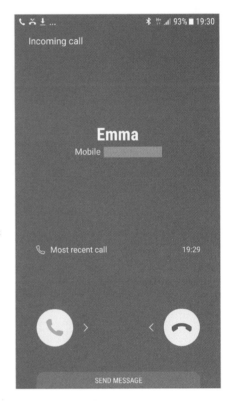

2 Swipe the green button to the right to accept a call, or swipe the red button to the left to reject it

3 If you are using another app when a call is received, the full-size window is minimized to a smaller one. Tap on **Answer**, or **Decline**

Incoming call

Emma
Mobile

ANSWER   DECLINE

SEND MESSAGE

4 Once a call has been accepted, these buttons appear at the bottom of the window, when in full screen

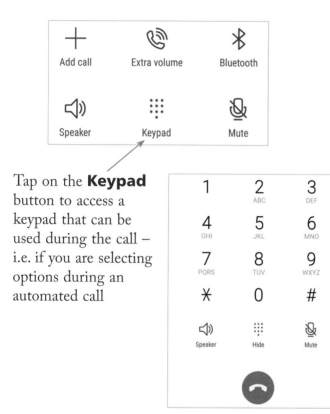

Tap on the **Bluetooth** button in Step 4 to connect your phone to a Bluetooth headset or headphones, so that you can take the call hands-free.

5 Tap on the **Keypad** button to access a keypad that can be used during the call – i.e. if you are selecting options during an automated call

6 Tap on the **Speaker** button to activate the speaker so that you can hear the call without holding the phone to your ear

7 The Home screen, or other apps, can be accessed during a call by pressing the Home

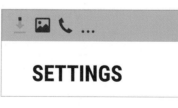

button, in which case the call window is minimized at the top of the screen

...cont'd

 8 During a call in full screen, tap on the **Menu** button at the top of the call window

9 Select options for the call, including putting it on **Hold**, viewing the caller in **View contact**, or **Send message**

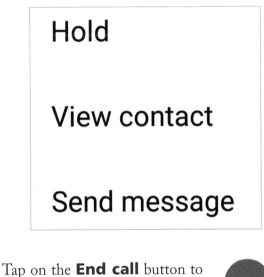

Hold

View contact

Send message

 10 Tap on the **End call** button to end the current call

11 Once a call has been ended, tap on these buttons to **View Contact** or call them back with a **Call**, **Message** or **Video call**

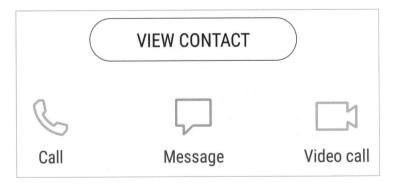

VIEW CONTACT

Call   Message   Video call

Setting Ringtones

Ringtones were one of the original must-have accessories that helped transform the way people looked at mobile/cell phones. Android phones have a range of ringtones that can be used, and you can also download and install thousands more. To use the default ringtones:

1 Tap on the **Settings** app

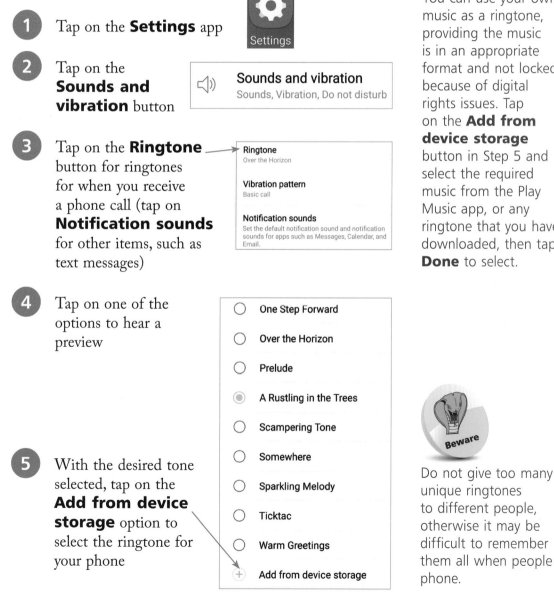

2 Tap on the **Sounds and vibration** button

🔊 **Sounds and vibration**
Sounds, Vibration, Do not disturb

3 Tap on the **Ringtone** button for ringtones for when you receive a phone call (tap on **Notification sounds** for other items, such as text messages)

Ringtone
Over the Horizon

Vibration pattern
Basic call

Notification sounds
Set the default notification sound and notification sounds for apps such as Messages, Calendar, and Email.

4 Tap on one of the options to hear a preview

○ One Step Forward

○ Over the Horizon

○ Prelude

◉ A Rustling in the Trees

○ Scampering Tone

○ Somewhere

○ Sparkling Melody

○ Ticktac

○ Warm Greetings

⊕ Add from device storage

5 With the desired tone selected, tap on the **Add from device storage** option to select the ringtone for your phone

Hot tip

You can use your own music as a ringtone, providing the music is in an appropriate format and not locked because of digital rights issues. Tap on the **Add from device storage** button in Step 5 and select the required music from the Play Music app, or any ringtone that you have downloaded, then tap **Done** to select.

Beware

Do not give too many unique ringtones to different people, otherwise it may be difficult to remember them all when people phone.

...cont'd

Getting more ringtones

While the default ringtones will serve a perfectly good purpose, there is also a wealth of sounds and music that can be downloaded and used as ringtones. This can be done through the Google Play Store:

Experimenting with different ringtones can be good fun, but after a while you may find that they can become slightly irritating for you, and those nearby.

1 Access the Google Play Store app. Tap on the Search box and enter **ringtones** to see the available options

Play Store

2 Tap on one of the search results

←	ringto**nes**	✕
Q	ringtones	
Q	ringtones **for android phone**	
Q	ringtones **free music**	

3 Tap on one of the ringtone apps to download it

ZEDGE™ Wallpapers & Ringtones
Zedge

Personalization   #1 Top Apps

INSTALL

4 Open the app and download one of the ringtones in the app. This will then be available in the list in Step 4 on page 97. Select it and tap on the **Add from device storage** button to use it as a ringtone

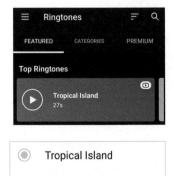

☰ Ringtones

FEATURED   CATEGORIES   PREMIUM

Top Ringtones

▶ Tropical Island
27s

◉ Tropical Island

◯ Warm Greetings

⊕ Add from device storage

6 Using the Keyboard

This chapter looks at entering text and data with the keyboard on an Android phone, focusing on the widely available Google keyboard: Gboard.

Keyboards with Android

All Android phones have a keyboard, for inputting text and data, and the vast majority of them are virtual ones – i.e. they appear on the screen, rather than an actual physical keyboard. Different phone manufacturers add their own keyboards to their specific handsets, and this is usually the default keyboard that appears. However, different keyboards can be downloaded from the Play Store, including the Google keyboard (Gboard), which is a good, multi-purpose Android keyboard. To download different keyboards:

Don't forget

As the Google keyboard is produced by Google, it can be considered the default Android keyboard and is used for the examples in this chapter.

100

 1   Access the
Play Store and
type **android
keyboard** into
the Search box

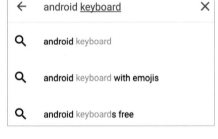

 2   Tap on one of
the search results
to view the
keyboard app
and download
and install it, if
required

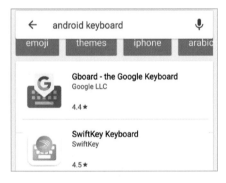

3   The keyboard app
will be added to
the next available
Home screen. Tap
on it to set it up
and also access its
settings once setup
is completed

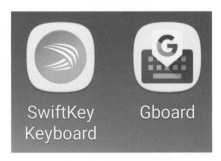

Selecting Keyboards

Several different keyboards can be installed and used on your Android phone. Keyboards can be changed at any time and different ones selected. To do this:

1 Tap on the **Settings** and select **General Management**

2 Tap on the **Language and input** option

3 Tap on the **Virtual keyboard** option

4 The available keyboards are listed. Tap on one to view its details and select it as the default

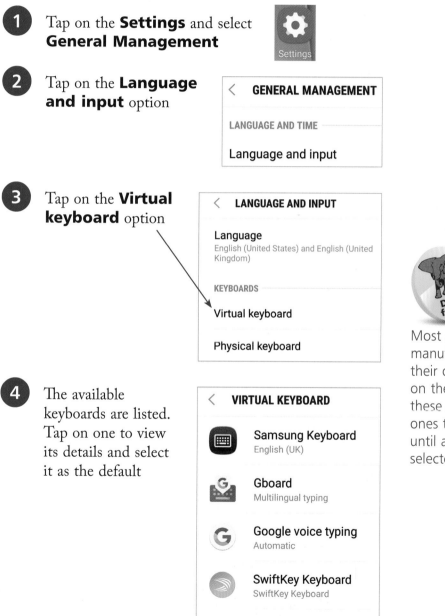

Don't forget

Most Android phone manufacturers include their own keyboards on their phones and these are the default ones that are used, until a different one is selected.

About the Google Keyboard

As with other Android keyboards, the Google keyboard (Gboard) can be used for a variety of actions:

- Entering text with a messaging app, word processing app, email app or a notes app.

- Entering a web address.

- Entering information into a form.

- Entering a password.

Viewing the keyboard

When you attempt one of the tasks above, the keyboard appears before you can enter any text or numbers:

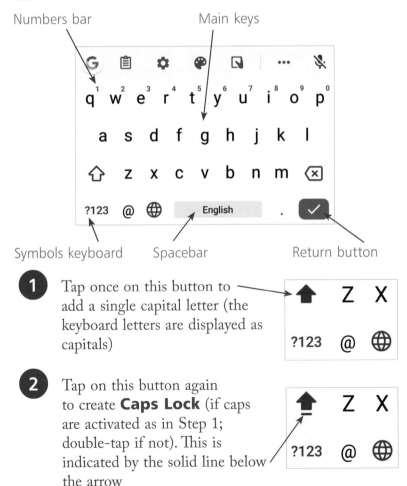

Numbers bar · Main keys

Symbols keyboard · Spacebar · Return button

1. Tap once on this button to add a single capital letter (the keyboard letters are displayed as capitals)

2. Tap on this button again to create **Caps Lock** (if caps are activated as in Step 1; double-tap if not). This is indicated by the solid line below the arrow

Don't forget

When using the keyboard for normal text or data entry, it only requires a light touch: you do not have to press very hard on the keys.

Don't forget

The Numbers bar on the Gboard is permanently available as part of the top row of letters: press and hold on a letter to add the number above it.

Don't forget

Caps Lock means that all the letters will be entered as capital letters.

3 Tap once on this button to back delete an item

4 Tap once on this button to access the **Symbols** keyboard option

?123

Hot tip

Tap on this button to access the number pad for entering numerical data.

1 2
3 4

Don't forget

Sometimes the button in Step 5 is **1/2** or **2/2**. Tap these buttons to move between the Symbols pages.

5 Tap on this button to access the second page of the **Symbols** keyboard

=\<

6 Tap once on this button on either of the symbols keyboards above to return to the standard **QWERTY** option

Hot tip

If you are entering a password, or details into a form, the keyboard will have a **Go** or **Send** button that can be used to activate the information that has been entered.

Keyboard Settings

There are a number of options for setting up the functionality of the Google keyboard. These can be accessed in two ways:

Tap on the **Preferences** button to access a range of options for the keys on the keyboard, and the layout and key press options such as for sounds and vibrations for when keys are pressed.

Most keyboards have a setting for **Predictive text**. This is a function where words are suggested as you type them: as more letters are added to the word, the suggestion becomes more defined. In the Gboard app, this functionality is provided by the **Show suggestion strip** option (see next page).

1 Tap on the **Gboard** app, or

2 Tap on the **Settings** button on the top shortcuts bar of the Google keyboard

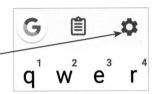

3 The full list of keyboard settings is displayed

4 Tap on the **Languages** option to select different languages

5 Tap on the **Theme** option to select a colored theme for the keyboard

6 Tap on the **Dictionary** option for creating a personal dictionary, which lets you add your own words to the dictionary, and also shortcuts for frequently used words or names

🌐	Languages English (US) (QWERTY), English (UK) (QWERTY)
🎚	Preferences
🎨	Theme
A̲	Text correction
🖉	Glide typing
🎤	Voice typing
▦	Dictionary
🔍	Search
⋯	Advanced
★	Rate us

7 Tap on the **Text correction** button shown on the previous page, to access options for working with text as it is being written

The **Show suggestion strip** option displays suggested words as you type (tap on one to select it); **Next-word suggestions** displays a possible next word, based on the one just used; **Show emoji suggestions** displays a suggested emoji to replace a word; and **Suggest Contacts** displays names from the Contacts app.

8 Drag **On** or **Off** the buttons for **Show suggestion strip**, **Next-word suggestions**, **Block offensive words**, **Show emoji suggestions** and **Suggest Contacts**

← Text correction

Suggestions

Show suggestion strip
Display suggestion strip while typing

Next-word suggestions
Use the previous word in making suggestions

Block offensive words
Do not suggest potentially offensive words

Show emoji suggestions

Suggest Contacts
Use information from Contacts for suggestions

Personalization
Adapt Gboard to your typing data and usage patterns

Corrections

9 Scroll down the **Text correction** page to access options for **Auto-correction**, **Autospace after punctuation**, **Auto-capitalization**, **Double-space period** and **Spell check.** Drag the buttons **On** or **Off** as required

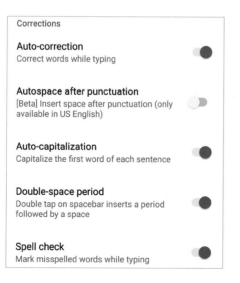

Corrections

Auto-correction
Correct words while typing

Autospace after punctuation
[Beta] Insert space after punctuation (only available in US English)

Auto-capitalization
Capitalize the first word of each sentence

Double-space period
Double tap on spacebar inserts a period followed by a space

Spell check
Mark misspelled words while typing

The **Auto-correction** option lets you insert the currently highlighted word by tapping on the spacebar; **Auto-capitalization** automatically inserts a capital letter at the start of a new sentence; **Double-space period** adds a period/full stop when the spacebar is tapped twice.

The Gboard app has been updated for Android 7.0 Nougat.

When a search result is shared using the **Share** button in Step 3, it is added to the current message, including a link to the web page from where the information was obtained.

Gboard Shortcuts Bar

At the top of the Gboard keyboard (and most other Android keyboards) is a shortcuts bar, if suggestions are turned on (see page 105). This includes the Google Search button and also additional functionality for the keyboard.

Google Search button

The Search button on the Gboard can be used for general search queries and also for finding information about the text message or email that you are writing:

1 Write a text message or email and tap on the **Google** Search button at the left-hand side of the Gboard shortcuts bar

2 Enter a search request and tap on the Search button on the keyboard

3 The search result is displayed. Tap on the **Share** and **View More** buttons as required

More shortcuts bar functionality

The Gboard shortcuts bar also has a range of other functionalities:

 Tap on this button to access **Stickers** to add to a message

 Tap on this button to select animated **GIF** images to add to a message

 Tap on this button to access the **Clipboard**, where items have been copied to

 Tap on this button to access the **Gboard Settings**

 Tap on this button to access more options for the shortcuts bar

 The additional options include: adding **Themes** to a message; using the keyboard **One-handed**; **Text Editing**; **Translate**; and **Floating**, which enables the keyboard to be moved around the screen

Voice typing can also be accessed from the shortcuts bar by tapping on this button.

If the **One-handed** option is selected in Step 6, the keyboard moves to the left or the right of the screen, so that it can more easily be accessed using just one hand.

107

For some items on the shortcuts bar, such as **Translate**, an item of text has to be selected for it to be active.

General Keyboard Shortcuts

Because of the size of the keyboard on an Android phone, some keys have duplicate functionality, in order to fit in all of the options. This includes dual function keys, spacebar shortcuts and accented letters.

Much of this functionality is accessed by pressing and holding on the keys, rather than just tapping on them once.

Dual functions
If a key has more than one character, both items can be accessed from the same button.

1 Press and hold on the period/full stop key to view the additional options. Slide your finger over the character, to insert it

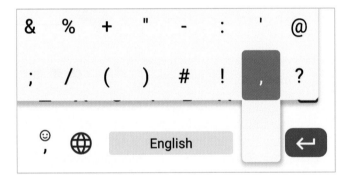

Spacebar shortcut
The spacebar can also be used for a useful shortcut: at the end of a

sentence, double-tap on the spacebar to add a full stop/period and a space, ready for the start of the next sentence, if this is enabled as shown in Step 9 on page 105.

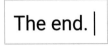

The end. |

Hot tip
Press and hold on compatible letters on the keyboard to access accented versions for different languages. These include the a, c, e, i, o, s and u keys.

Adding Text

Once you have applied the keyboard settings that you require, you can start entering text, in appropriate apps:

1 Tap once in a text box to activate the keyboard. Start typing with the keyboard. The text will appear at the point where you tapped on the screen

2 If **Show suggestion strip** is enabled, suggestions appear above the keyboard as you type a word. Tap once on a word on the suggestions strip to include it

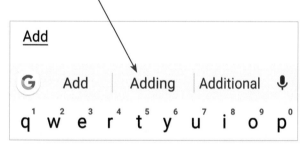

3 If **Next-word suggestions** is enabled, suggestions appear after the last word entered

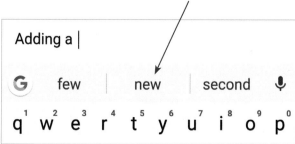

Use the back delete button to remove unwanted text once it has been added.

If **Show suggestion strip** is enabled in the keyboard settings (see page 105), **Next-word suggestions** is automatically enabled.

For details about adding text in a text message, see pages 112-113.

Working with Text

Once text has been entered it can be selected, copied, cut and pasted, either within an app or between apps.

Selecting text

To select text and perform tasks on it:

Don't forget

The Format button shown in Steps 5 and 6 can be used to apply formatting options to the selected text, including bold and italics, depending on the app being used.

Don't forget

To select all of the text in a text box, press and hold on the text, then tap on the **Select All** button in Step 6.

 1   Tap anywhere to set the insertion point for adding or editing text

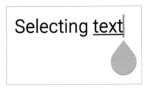

2   Drag the marker to move the insertion point

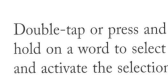

3   Double-tap or press and hold on a word to select it and activate the selection handles

 4   Drag the handles to change the text that is selected

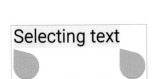

5   Tap on these buttons to cut or copy the selected text

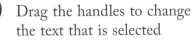

FORMAT   CUT   COPY   ⋮

 6   Locate the point at which you want to insert the text, and press and hold. Tap on **Paste** to add the text

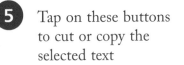

FORMAT   PASTE   SELECT ALL

7 Messaging and Email

This chapter shows how to keep in touch using text messages, and how to enhance them with emojis and attachments.

Texting Contacts

As with phone calls, it is possible to use your contacts to send text messages in a number of ways:

Finding a contact in Messages

To text a contact directly from the Messages app:

When you send a text message to someone this starts a conversation thread. To delete a thread, in the **Messages** app, press and hold on the conversation thread, and tap on the **Delete** option at the top of the window.

Don't forget

Apps such as WhatsApp and Messenger (Facebook) can be used for texting people. This is known as "internet messaging", and one of its useful features is being able to create text groups, so that everyone in a group can see what the other members are saying. It is usually free to message people with these apps.

1 Tap on the **Messages** app

2 Tap on the **New message** button

3 In the **Contacts** section, tap here to select a recipient for the message

4 Tap on the required name to select it and tap on the **Compose** button

5 Enter the text for the message

6 Compose the text and tap on the **Send** button

Texting from your Contacts list

You can also text a contact directly from your Contacts list:

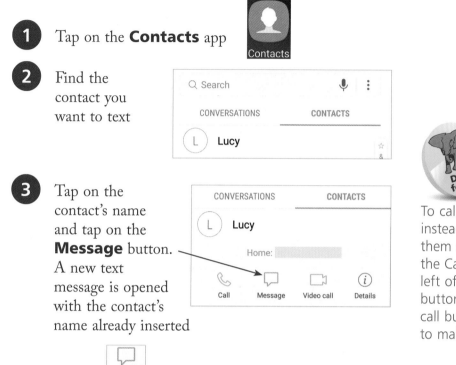

1 Tap on the **Contacts** app

2 Find the contact you want to text

3 Tap on the contact's name and tap on the **Message** button. A new text message is opened with the contact's name already inserted

Quick contact messaging

As with a phone call, it is possible to quickly start a text message with a contact with one swipe. To do this:

1 Tap on the **Contacts** app

2 Find the contact you want to text

3 Swipe to the left on the contact's name. The orange **Message** button appears and opens up a new text message with the contact's name already inserted as the recipient

Use emojis sparingly, as the novelty can soon wear off for the recipient.

Beware

Emojis can also be added to emails and any apps where the emoji keyboard is available.

Using Emojis

Emojis (small graphical symbols) are now a common sight in text messages and on social media. Some people love them, while others loathe them, but they are now a regular feature in digital communications.

Emojis can be inserted directly from the Messages text box:

 Compose a text message, and at any point, tap on the emoji symbol next to the message

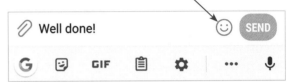

 The default category of emojis is displayed. Tap on an item to add it to a message

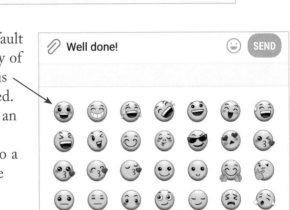

3 Tap on this button to view the most recently used emoji

4 Tap on the buttons on the bottom toolbar to view the emojis' different categories

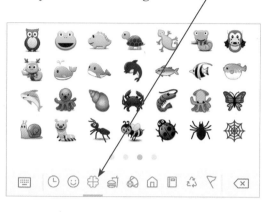

The range of emojis on the Gboard app has been updated for Android 7.0 Nougat.

5 Swipe left and right, or tap on the buttons below the emojis, to view all of the emojis in a category. Tap on an emoji to add it

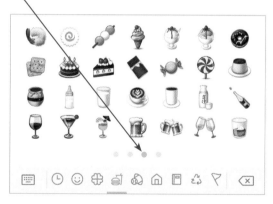

Don't forget

The functionality in Step 6 can be activated by turning **On** the **Show emoji suggestions** option in the **Text correction** section of the keyboard settings. See page 105 for details.

6 When writing a message, emojis will appear on the shortcuts bar when they match a word that has been entered. Tap on the emoji to replace the word

Adding Attachments

Text messages do not have to only include words; it is also possible to attach a variety of other items, such as photos, music tracks and videos:

1 Open a new text message and tap on the **Attach** button

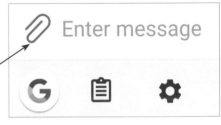

2 Select the location from where you want to add the attachment

3 For the **Gallery** option (or **Photos** on some models), where all of

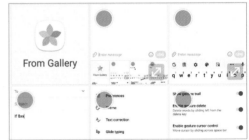

your photos are stored, tap on one of the images to add it to the message

4 For the **Other** option, select the type of media to be added to the message – e.g. video or an audio file

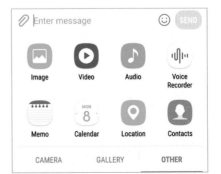

Glide Typing

Another way of creating texts with the Google keyboard is with the Glide typing option. This is where you swipe over the keyboard to create words, rather than tapping on the individual letters. To do this:

 1 Select **Settings > General Management > Language and input > Virtual keyboard > Gboard** and tap on the **Glide typing** option

2 Drag the **Enable glide typing** and **Show gesture trail** buttons to **On**

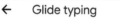

← Glide typing

Enable glide typing
Input a word by sliding through the letters

Show gesture trail

 3 When you create a message, drag over the keyboard with a finger to add the letters for the words you want to create. If the **Show gesture trail** option in Step 2 is **On**, a colored line is visible as your finger moves over the letters. If you need to create a double letter, make a circular motion on the relevant letter on the keyboard

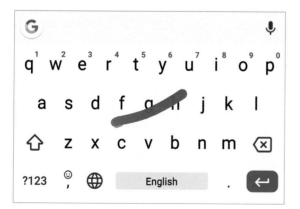

Beware

Glide typing is best used for short messages, rather than trying to write anything of length.

Setting Up Email

Email is still one of the main forms of electronic communication. Most Android phone manufacturers include their own email app for adding email accounts, but the Gmail app can also be used for this, in addition to being used for emails from a Google Account. To add an email account:

Don't forget

Email accounts can also be set up from the Settings app, under **iCloud and accounts** > **Accounts** > **Add account**.

Hot tip

Usually, email providers have their own apps – e.g. Outlook.com for Microsoft accounts; Yahoo! Mail; etc.

1 Tap on the **Gmail** app

2 Tap on the Gmail **Menu** button in the top left-hand corner

≡   Search mail

3 Swipe down the menu and tap on the **Settings** button

⚙   Settings

4 Tap on the **Add account** option to add a new account that can be used with the Gmail app

←   Settings

General settings

nickvandome@googlemail.com

Add account

5 Tap on the type of account that you want to add. Tap on the **Other** option if your email account provider is not on the list

M

Set up email

G   Google

O   Outlook, Hotmail, and Live

✉   Yahoo

E   Exchange and Office 365

✉   Other

6 Enter the email address of the account you want to add, and then tap on the **Next** button

Add your email address

Enter your email
nickvandome@mac.com|

MANUAL SETUP   NEXT

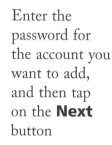

Numerous email accounts can be added to the Gmail app.

7 Enter the password for the account you want to add, and then tap on the **Next** button

M

nickvandome@mac.com

Password
········| 👁️‍🗨️

NEXT

When an email account is synced, any items that are saved online are copied to the phone, so that the two locations display the same information.

8 Select the options for the account, including those for notifications when emails arrive; syncing the account; and downloading attachments. Tap on the **Next** button to finish setting up the new account

Account options

Sync frequency:

Every 15 minutes   ▼

☑ Notify me when email arrives

☑ Sync email from this account

☑ Automatically download attachments when connected to Wi-Fi

NEXT

Using Gmail

Accessing emails

Emails from different email accounts can all be viewed and managed using Gmail. To do this:

1 Tap on the **Gmail** app

2 By default, Gmail should open at your Inbox, with your emails displayed. Tap on one to open it. Tap on the Menu button to view the mailbox options

Hot tip

Swipe down from the top of the Inbox to manually refresh it.

3 Tap on the **Inbox** button to return to your Inbox at any point. Tap on the other options to view folders with specific items, such as **Sent** mail and any **Drafts** you have written

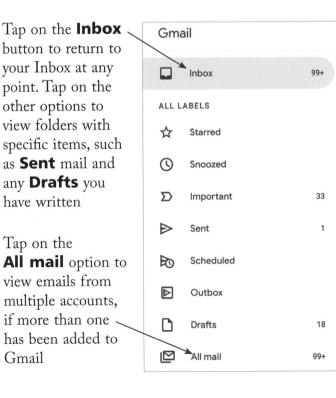

4 Tap on the **All mail** option to view emails from multiple accounts, if more than one has been added to Gmail

Creating email

Once you have set up an email account you can use it to send and receive all of your emails on your Android phone. To send an email:

1 Tap on the **Gmail** app

2 Tap on the **Compose** button

3 Compose the email by adding a recipient, subject and body text

←	Compose	📎 ▷ ⋮
From	nickvandome@googlemail.com	
To	eilidhvandome@gmail.co...	⌄
Job		
Hi, how's the new job going?		

4 To format text, press on a word to select it. Tap on the **Format** button to access the formatting toolbar

J   FORMAT   CUT   COPY   ⋮

Hi, how's the new job going?

5 Select the required formatting for the selected word, including bold, italics, underlining, text color, background text color and strikethrough

Hi, how's the new job going?

B *I* U A ◆. ✗ ×

6 When you have finished composing your email, tap on the **Send** button

Hot tip

If a recipient is in your Contacts app, their full email address will appear as you type their name in Step 3, providing the email address is included in their entry in the Contacts app.

Hot tip

Tap on the **Attach** button on the top bar to include photos, video or music files in your email.

121

Going Hands-free

If you do not want to bother fiddling around with fingers and thumbs to create your messages, you can use Speech mode instead:

1 Open a new text message or email and tap on the microphone button

2 When the **Speak now** window appears, speak your message as clearly as possible

Speak now

3 As you are speaking, the **Listening...** window appears

Listening...

4 Your words will be converted into text

How are you today

SEND

Listening...

Beware

Creating text with the microphone is not an exact science and you may find that you end up with some strange interpretations of your words.

8 Android Apps

The functionality on an Android phone is provided by its apps. This chapter details the pre-installed ones, and shows how to download more and update them. It also looks at some of the most common apps, covering maps, notes, social media, health and fitness, and games.

Apps for Android

An app is just a more modern name for a computer program. The terminology first became widely used on smartphones, but has now spread to all forms of computing and is firmly embedded in the language of phones.

On Android phones there are three types of apps:

- **Generic apps** – Come pre-installed on your Android phone. In general, these apps are specific to the manufacturer of the phone.

- **Google apps** – Downloaded from the online Play Store. Google apps are compatible with the same apps on other Google devices. A number of these apps are also pre-installed on a lot of Android phones.

- **Apps from other developers** – Non-Google apps, downloaded from the Play Store.

Generic apps

The types of generic apps that are available on Android phones include:

- **Calculator**. A standard calculator that also has some scientific functions, although not the range of a full scientific calculator.

- **Calendar**. An app for storing appointments, important dates and other calendar information.

- **Camera**. Android smartphones have at least one camera and most have two: a front-facing and back-facing one. These can be accessed from the Camera app.

- **Clock**. This can be used to view the time in different countries, and also functions as an alarm clock, a timer, and a stopwatch.

- **Contacts**. The Contacts app serves as an address book where you can enter details about your friends and family members. Calls and texts can be sent directly from the app.

Because of the open source nature of Android, manufacturers can customize the built-in apps for their devices.

Most apps have menu options that can be accessed from the buttons below (some apps have both, but they provide the same menu functionality).

124

- **Email**. A lot of Android phones have a generic email app, which can be used to link to your email accounts. However, the Gmail app also serves this purpose.

Email

- **Fitness**. Health and fitness is increasingly popular on smartphones, and most Android phones have an app for measuring activity.

Samsung Health

Don't forget

Health and fitness apps record details for areas including number of steps taken, calories consumed, heart rate, and workout activity.

- **Internet**. Although a generic Internet app is included with a lot of Android phones, the Google Chrome app is probably the best option for accessing the web.

Internet

- **Messages**. This is the generic app for sending text messages, which is done through your 3G/4G cellular network.

Messages

- **Phone**. This is the generic app for making calls (and accessing contacts for calls), video calls and sending text messages.

Phone

- **Photos**. In addition to the Camera app, some Android phones have a Photos app that can be used to view, manage, edit and share photos, and other models feature a Gallery app.

Gallery

- **Play Store**. Although this is a Google app, it is included on most Android phones so that you can access the Play Store for downloading apps, books, music, movies and magazines.

Play Store

Don't forget

In addition to the Play Store, some phone manufacturers also offer their own app stores, although the range of apps is usually more limited.

- **Notes/Memos**. Notes and memo apps are provided on most Android phones, and they are useful for jotting down items such as shopping lists and packing lists for traveling.

Memo

- **Settings**. This contains all of the settings that can be applied to the phone so you can customize it to the way you want.

Settings

Google Apps

Most Android phones come with some Google apps already pre-installed. If not, the apps can be downloaded from the Play Store. The Google apps for Android phones include:

- **Chrome**. Different Android phones have different types of browsers for accessing the web. The Chrome browser is the default on some phones.

- **Docs**. This can be used to create word processing documents and keep them in cloud storage (online storage) or on your phone.

- **Drive**. This app provides online storage and backup for documents and files on your phone, stored by Google.

- **Gmail**. When you set up a Google Account you will also create a Gmail account for sending and receiving email. This app can be used for accessing and using your Gmail.

- **Google**. This app can be used for accessing the Google Search function – still one of the best search facilities available. It can also be used for accessing the Google Discover function.

- **Hangouts**. This is a Google social media app that can be used to chat with friends, using either text or video, and share photos.

- **Maps**. The Google Maps app is one of the best mapping apps available for finding locations and obtaining directions.

- **Play Books**. This is the app for reading ebooks on an Android phone. It can be used to manage books in your library and also download new ones from the Play Store.

Hot tip

Messages from the Hangouts app can be replied to directly from the Notification panel, without having to first open the app.

- **Play Games**. This is the app for accessing games from the Play Store and playing them on your phone.

- **Play Movies & TV**. Another app linked to the Play Store. It is used to view movies that you have bought or rented from the Play Store and to view your own personal videos.

- **Play Music**. This is the default music player that can be used to play your own music and also music content from the Play Store.

- **News**. This is a news app that collates stories on specific topics, or from certain publications.

- **Sheets**. This can be used to create spreadsheets and keep them in cloud storage (online storage) or on your phone.

- **Slides**. This can be used to create presentations and keep them in cloud storage (online storage) or on your phone.

- **Voice Search**. This is Google's app for searching for items by speaking. Tap on the app and then speak your search query.

- **YouTube**. This is the popular video-sharing app that is now owned by Google. It can be used to view millions of videos covering most subjects imaginable.

Some Android phones have different apps for functions such as playing music and movies, and reading books and magazines. If this is the case, the Play apps here can still be downloaded from the Play Store.

Maps

The default maps app on Android phones is Google Maps, one of the best mapping apps on the market. It can be used to view locations, get directions and view transit details.

When viewing a map in Step 2, tap on this button to tilt the perspective of the map.
Tap on this button to return to the default view.

1 Tap on the **Maps** app

2 The current location is displayed (if **Location** is enabled under **Settings > Connections**). Double-tap with one finger to zoom in; double-tap with two fingers to zoom out. Swipe outwards with thumb and forefinger to zoom in; pinch inwards to zoom out

3 To view other locations, type a place name, address, zip/postcode or landmark in the Search box at the top of the window. Results are displayed as you type

4 Tap on one of the results to view a map of it. Some locations also have additional features such as photos. Tap on an item to view it, or swipe up from the bottom of the window to view more details about a location and questions that have been asked about it

Getting directions

The Maps app is very effective in providing directions between two points. To do this:

1 Tap on the **Go** button

2 Enter the starting point and destination for the directions in the text fields at the top of the window (by default, the starting point is your current location but this can be changed by tapping in the field and entering a new location for the starting point). The route is displayed on the map. Tap the **Menu** button to add a stop, and for more options

3 Tap on these buttons to select the mode of transport for the journey

4 Tap on the **Start** button to view step-by-step directions for the journey

5 As you change your location the map updates accordingly and gives you spoken directions. Tap the speaker button for options to turn off spoken directions (mute) or to hear alerts only

Hot tip

Tap on the **Menu** button on the bottom toolbar, when viewing a location on a map, to access the options, such as adding the route to the Home screen and displaying all traffic.

Route options	
Add stop	
Set depart or arrive time	
Add route to Home screen	
Share directions	
Share your location	
All traffic	☐
Satellite	☐
Terrain	☐

Notes and Memos

Taking notes on an Android phone is an excellent way to keep up-to-date with a range of tasks, from shopping lists to reminders for packing for a trip. There are several notes and memos apps that can be downloaded from the Play Store, and most smartphone manufacturers include a default notes and memos app. The example here uses the Samsung Memo app. To use it:

1 Tap on the **Memo** app

2 Tap on this button to create a new memo

3 Enter a title for the memo and the text for the memo

4 Once the memo is completed, tap on the **Save** button

5 The memo is added to the **All memos** Homepage

6 Each time a new memo is added, it is listed at the top of the **All memos** page. Tap on a memo to view it and edit it, if required

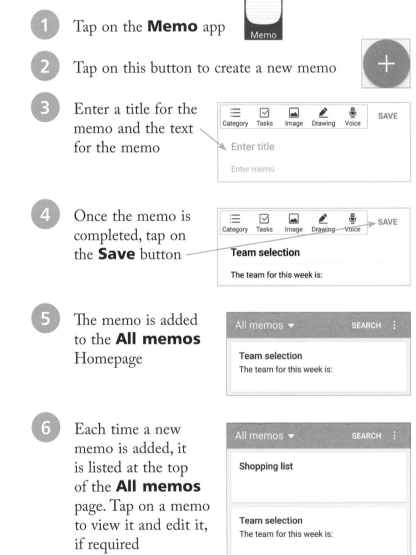

Hot tip

When creating a new memo or note, tap on these buttons at the top of the window to, from left to right, add a new category for memos; add checkboxes for tasks add images; draw on a note; or record a voice recording.

Social Media

Social media has transformed the way in which we communicate, and there are numerous apps that can be used on an Android phone for social media. These can be downloaded from the **Play Store**, from within the **Social** category. Some of the most popular apps are:

Facebook

This is still one of the most widely used social media tools. To use Facebook you have to first register, which is free. You can then link up with your friends and share a variety of content, by searching for them and inviting them to join your network with a Friend Request.

Twitter

Twitter is a microblogging site where users post short messages (tweets). Once you have joined Twitter, which is free, you can follow other users to see what they are saying and have people follow you too.

Snapchat

Snapchat is a messaging service that allows users to send photos and videos to their Snapchat friends, or groups of people. Once these are accessed, they remain visible for a few seconds and then they are deleted. Text and graphics can be added to items when they are sent – one of the most frequent uses is for sending self-portraits ("selfies" – see page 162).

Pinterest

This is an online pinboard, where you can bookmark and "pin" items of interest, and upload your own content for other people to pin.

Instagram

This is a popular photo- and video-sharing site. Followers can be added by users and they can then comment and "like" photos. By default, the security settings are for public viewing of content, so these should be changed if you only want your own followers to be able to view your content.

YouTube is one of the great successes of the internet age. It is a video-sharing site, with millions of video clips covering every subject imaginable. There is a built-in YouTube app on most Android phones, which can be accessed from the All Apps button.

YouTube

Health and Fitness

Monitoring health and fitness with digital devices is a growth industry and there is also a range of health and fitness apps that can record exercise activity on your Android phone. One of these is the Google Fit app. To use this:

The Google Fit app can be downloaded from the Play Store, as can a range of health and fitness apps.

Tap on the **Add activity** button in Step 3 to manually add details of an activity that has not been recorded by the app on the phone.

Once an activity has been paused as in Step 5, tap on the **Play** button (below, right) to restart it, or the **Stop** button (below, left) to save the activity details within the app.

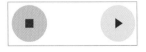

1. Tap on the **Fit** app

2. Tap on this button to enter health and fitness information or start a new activity

3. Select an option from the menu – e.g. **Add activity**. This can be used for entering data for an activity that you have already undertaken

Add blood pressure	
Add weight	
Add activity	
Track workout	

4. Select the type of activity that you want to record, and tap on the **Save** button

5. If **Track workout** is selected in Step 3, tap on the **Start** button to begin recording the workout activity. Tap on the **Pause** button to pause the workout recording

Playing Games

Although computer games may seem like the preserve of the younger generation, this is definitely not the case. Not all computer games are of the shoot-em-up or racing variety, and the Play Store also contains puzzles and versions of popular board games. Some games to try are:

- **Chess**. Pit your wits against this Chess app. Various settings can be applied for each game, such as the level of difficulty.

- **Checkers**. Similar to the Chess app, but for Checkers (Draughts). Hints are also available to help develop your skills and knowledge.

- **Mahjong**. A version of the popular Chinese game, this is a matching game for single players, rather than playing with other people.

- **Scrabble**. An Android phone version of the best-selling word game that can be played with up to four people.

- **Solitaire**. An old favorite, the card game where you have to build sequences and remove all of the cards.

- **Sudoku**. The logic game where you have to fill different grids with numbers 1-9, without having any of the same number in a row or column.

- **Tetris**. One of the original computer games, where you have to piece together falling shapes to make lines.

- **Words With Friends**. Similar to Scrabble, an online word game, played with other users.

As well as the games here, there is a full range of other types of games in the Play Store, which can be accessed from the **Games** category. They can also be accessed from the **Play Games** app.

Play Games

Around the Play Store

Although the pre-installed apps provide a lot of useful functionality and are a good starting point, the Play Store is where you can really start to take advantage of the wide range of apps that are available. These can be used for entertainment, communication, productivity and much more.

To access the Play Store and find apps:

New apps are added to the Play Store on a regular basis (and existing ones are updated), so the Homepage will change appearance regularly.

1 Tap on the **Play Store** app

2 Suggested items are shown on the Play Store Homepage, under the **For You** heading

App prices are shown in the local currency.

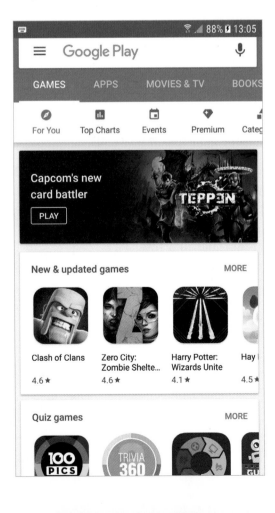

3 Swipe up and down
or left and right to
see the full range of
recommendations for
all types of content in
the Play Store. Tap on
an item to view further
details about it

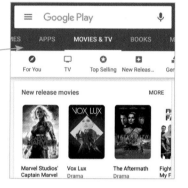

Tap on the **More**
button from a section
on the Homepage to
view additional items.

MORE

4 Use these buttons to
find relevant content:
Games, **Apps**,
Movies & TV, **Books**
or **Music**

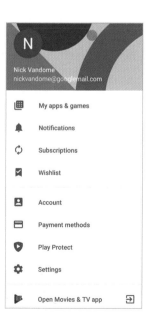

5 Tap on the **Menu** button to
access the Play Store menu

135

Finding Apps

Searching by category

When you have accessed the Play Store you can then look for content in a variety of ways:

136

1 The featured and recommended items are displayed on the Homepage (by default, this opens on the **Games** section). Swipe up and down and left and right to view the full range, and tap on an item to view more details

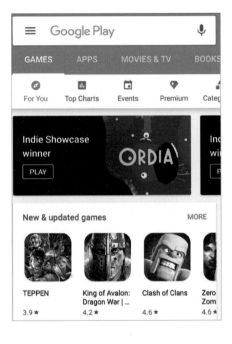

2 Tap on the **Apps** tab to view the available range of apps. Swipe left and right on the top bar to view apps according to **For You**, **Top Charts**, **Categories**, **Editors' Choice**, **Family**, and **Early Access**

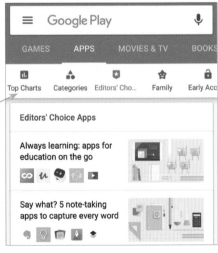

3 Tap on the **Categories** tab in Step 2 on the previous page, and tap on a category to view the apps according to the relevant headings

4 Search for apps within a category in the same way as for searching over the whole range of apps, as in Step 2 on the previous page

Using the Search box

1 Tap in the Google Play Search box on any page to conduct a search with keywords

2 Enter the name of the item for which you want to search

3 Tap on one of the suggested results, or tap on this button on the keyboard to conduct another search

Don't forget

As you type in the Search box, the suggested items will change, depending on the keyword(s) used.

Downloading Apps

Once you have found an app in the Play Store that you want to use, you can download it to your phone:

1 Access the app you want to use. There will be details about the app and reviews from other users if you scroll down the page

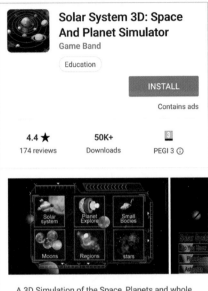

2 Tap on the **Install** button, and the app will start downloading

3 Tap on the **Open** button to open the app once it has finished downloading and installing

4 Some apps require the user to accept their terms and conditions of usage. Tap on the **Accept** button to accept and continue using the app

 5 Some apps will also request permission for items such as accessing your location. Tap **Allow** or **Deny** as required

Don't forget

If an app has access to your device's location it creates more location-specific content. If you deny an app permissions, it may not work.

139

Allow **NASA** to access this device's location?

DENY   ALLOW

6 Newly downloaded apps usually appear on the next available All Apps screen where there is a space. From here, the app can be opened and also moved to another location. A shortcut on your Home screen is sometimes also created

Uninstalling Apps

The pre-installed apps on an Android phone cannot be deleted easily (although they can be turned off), but the ones that have been downloaded from the Play Store can be uninstalled. You may want to do this if you do not use a certain app any more, or you feel the number of apps on your phone is becoming too great. To uninstall a downloaded app:

If apps are selected in the same way as in Step 1 from any Home screen, the available button is **Remove shortcut.** Drag the app over this button to remove it from the Remove shortcut Home screen, but it will still be available from the All Apps section. Built-in apps cannot be uninstalled, but they can be removed from the Home screen.

1 Access the **All Apps** section and press and hold on one of the apps until the **Uninstall** button appears

2 Drag the app over the **Uninstall** button until it turns red, and release to uninstall the app

If apps have been uninstalled from the phone, they can be reinstalled from the Play Store app by selecting **My apps & games** from the main menu and tapping on the **Library** option to view all of the apps that have previously been downloaded.

3 Tap on the **OK** button to confirm the uninstall

Solar System 3D

Do you want to uninstall this app?

CANCEL   OK

Turning off built-in apps

Pre-installed apps cannot be uninstalled easily, but they can be turned off so that they cannot be used. This is done from the All Apps area, in a similar way for uninstalling apps:

1. Press and hold the app to be turned off. Tap on the **Disable** button

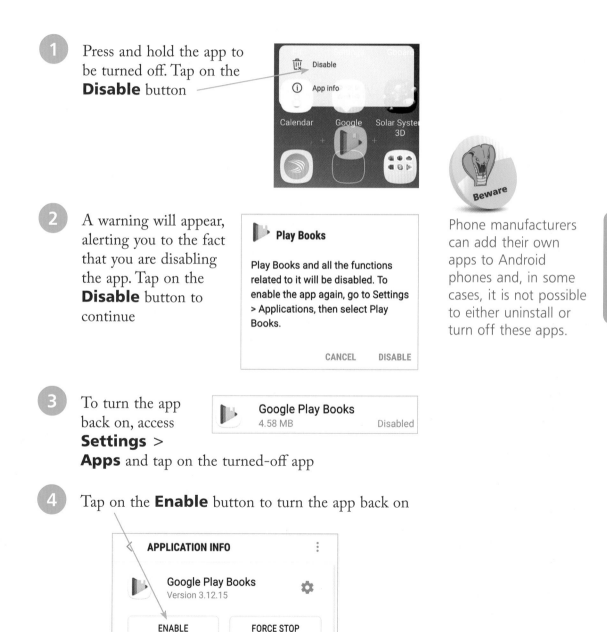

2. A warning will appear, alerting you to the fact that you are disabling the app. Tap on the **Disable** button to continue

Phone manufacturers can add their own apps to Android phones and, in some cases, it is not possible to either uninstall or turn off these apps.

3. To turn the app back on, access **Settings** > **Apps** and tap on the turned-off app

4. Tap on the **Enable** button to turn the app back on

Updating Apps

The world of apps is a dynamic and fast-moving one, and new apps are being created and added to the Play Store on a daily basis. Existing apps are also being updated, to improve their performance and functionality. These can be added to your phone either automatically or manually:

Updating apps automatically

Hot tip

Apps are also updated to improve security features and include any fixes to improve the performance of the app.

142

1 Access the Play Store. Tap on the **Menu** button and then the **Settings** button

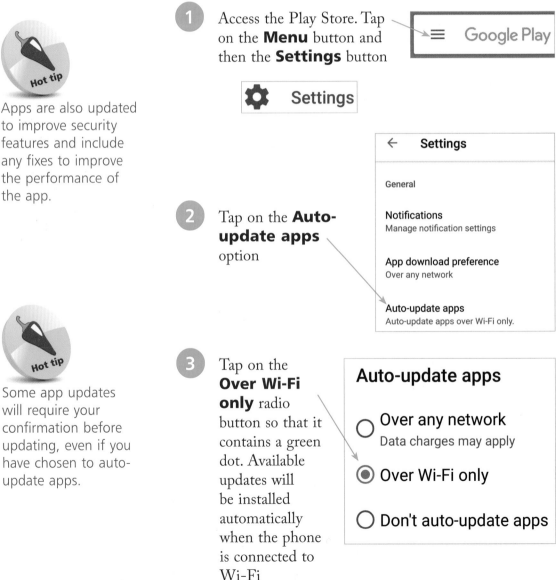

2 Tap on the **Auto-update apps** option

Hot tip

Some app updates will require your confirmation before updating, even if you have chosen to auto-update apps.

3 Tap on the **Over Wi-Fi only** radio button so that it contains a green dot. Available updates will be installed automatically when the phone is connected to Wi-Fi

…cont'd

Updating apps manually

Apps can also be updated manually:

1 Ensure **Don't auto-update apps** is selected in Step 3 on the previous page

⊙ Don't auto-update apps

DONE

2 Access the Play Store. Tap on the **Menu** button and then the **My apps & games** option

≡ Google Play

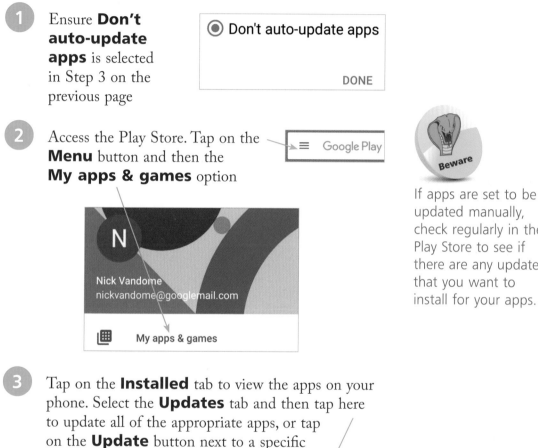

N

Nick Vandome
nickvandome@googlemail.com

⊞ My apps & games

3 Tap on the **Installed** tab to view the apps on your phone. Select the **Updates** tab and then tap here to update all of the appropriate apps, or tap on the **Update** button next to a specific app to update it

← My apps & games

UPDATES   INSTALLED   LIBRARY

Updates available (1)
Auto-update is turned off   UPDATE ALL

SmartThings
40 MB   UPDATE

If apps are set to be updated manually, check regularly in the Play Store to see if there are any updates that you want to install for your apps.

143

App Information

For both pre-installed apps and those downloaded from the Play Store, it is possible to view details about them and also see the permissions that they are using to access certain functions. To view information about your apps:

1 Open the **Settings** app and tap on the **Apps** button

2 Tap on an app to select it and view its details

Tap on the **Notifications** button in the **Application Info** window to specify how notifications are handled for the app. Drag the **Allow notifications** button to **On** to enable notifications to be displayed for the app.

3 Tap on the **Force Stop** button to close a running app

4 Tap on the **Mobile data** button to view details about the size of the app, and the amount of data it has stored

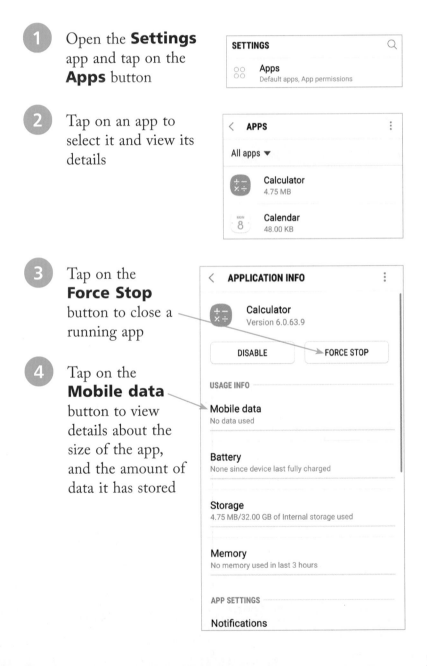

9 Being Entertained

Android phones are not only useful, they are also great fun. This chapter shows how to use your phone for playing music, watching movies and reading books.

For details about opening web pages, see page 175.

Content that is downloaded to your Android phone via the Play Store will also be available on the Google Play website, as long as you are logged in with your Google Account.

If you buy music from either the Play Store or the Google Play website, it can be played on your phone with streaming (using a Wi-Fi internet connection – see page 150) or it can be downloaded (pinned) onto your phone so that you can also listen to it offline (see pages 154-155).

The Google Play Website

Google Play is Google's online store for buying, downloading, using and managing a range of entertainment content. It is accessed at the website:

- **play.google.com**

You need to have a Google Account in order to log in to the Google Play website. Once you have logged in to Google Play you can download a variety of content:

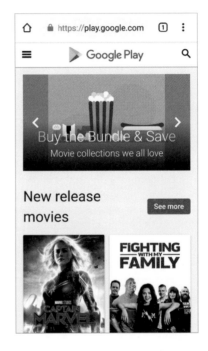

- Music
- Movies and TV shows
- Apps
- Ebooks

Content from Google Play is stored in the cloud so it can then be used on your computer and also your Android phone. If you delete it from your phone, either accidentally or on purpose, you can still reinstall it from Google Play. You can also use content downloaded by any of your other Android devices, such as a tablet.

Music on Android

One option for playing music on an Android phone is the Google Play Music app. It can be used to play music that has been obtained in a number of different ways:

Play Music

- Downloaded directly to your phone from the **Play Store**.

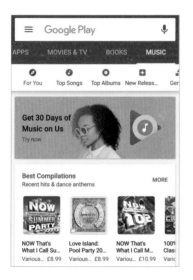

- Bought on **Google Play** and then used on another device.

- Transferred from your computer directly to your phone. This is done by connecting your phone to your computer, using the USB cable, and copying your music to the **Music** folder on your phone, and then locating the music files through the Play Music app.

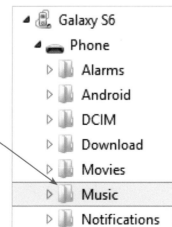

- Transferred from another mobile device using Bluetooth.

Don't forget

Google Play Music also offers a subscription service that enables users to download unlimited music through the Play Music app or the Google Play Store. There is a standard 30-day free trial (some phone manufacturers offer a longer free trial of Play Music), with options for either individual or family memberships after the free period finishes. Google Play Music can be joined when you first open the Play Music app.

Downloading Music

To use your phone directly to find and download music from the Play Store:

In some cases, there may be sample content in the Play Music app to help you get started with playing music.

1 Tap on the **Play Music** app to open the music player

2 Tap on the **Menu** button to access the Play Music menu, and tap on the **Shop** button

Listen Now

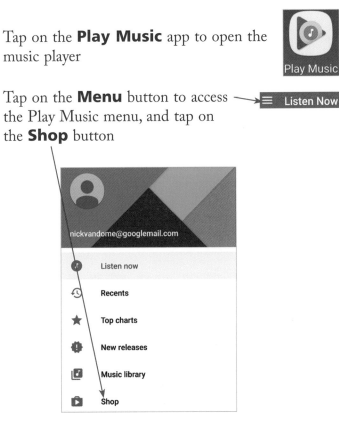

nickvandome@googlemail.com

Listen now

Recents

Top charts

New releases

Music library

Shop

3 Use these buttons to view the relevant sections within the Music section of the Play Store, or

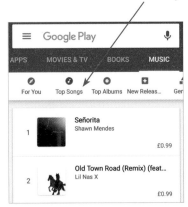

≡ Google Play

APPS   MOVIES & TV   BOOKS   **MUSIC**

For You   Top Songs   Top Albums   New Releas...   Ger

1   Señorita
Shawn Mendes
£0.99

2   Old Town Road (Remix) (feat...
Lil Nas X
£0.99

4 Enter an artist, album or song name into the Search box

5 Locate the item you want to download. For an album, tap on this button to buy the full album,

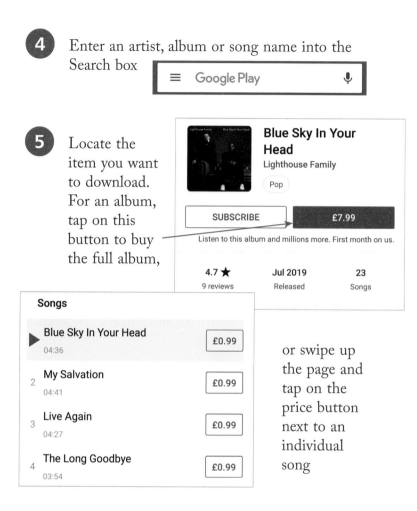

When you buy music from the Play Store it also comes with the related artwork such as album or singles covers.

or swipe up the page and tap on the price button next to an individual song

6 Tap on the **Buy** button and enter your Google Account password to buy the item and download it to your phone

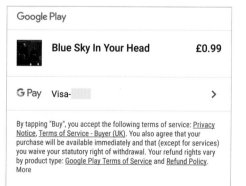

Playing Music

Once you have obtained music on your phone, by whatever means, you can then start playing it and listening to it. To do this:

Don't forget

If the Music library is not displayed when you open the Play Music app, tap on the **Menu** button and tap on the **Music library** button.

Don't forget

Streaming is a process where digital content is sent to a device over Wi-Fi when it is needed, in order for it to be played continuously on the device. It does not physically download the content onto the device and it remains on the server from where it was streamed.

1 Tap on the **Play Music** app

2 All of the available music is displayed. This includes music from the Play Music store that is only available for streaming at this point – i.e. it needs a Wi-Fi connection to play it

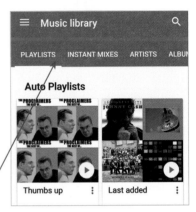

3 Tap on these buttons to view your music content according to **Playlists**, **Instant Mixes**, **Artists**, **Albums**, **Songs** and **Genres**

4 Tap on an item to view the available songs (for an album) or individual tracks

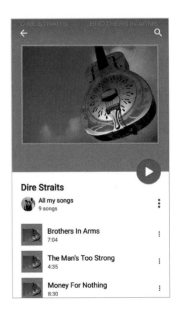

Tap on a song to play it. The currently playing song is also displayed at the bottom of the Play Music app

 Tap on the song or album icon to view the song artwork at full size, and view the standard playback controls at the bottom of the window

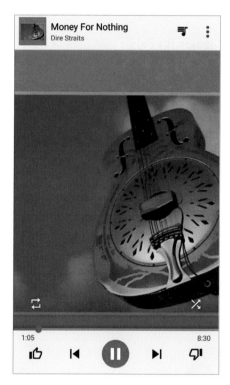

Hot tip

Invest in a reasonable set of headphones to listen to music on your Android phone. This will usually result in a higher-quality sound than through the built-in speakers.

151

 When a song is playing, this button appears next to it

The Man's Too Strong
4:35

Money For Nothing
8:30

One World
3:38

...cont'd

Music controls
When a song is playing there are several options:

 Use these buttons to, from left to right: go back to the beginning of a song; pause/play a song; 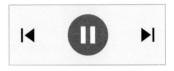 go to the end of a song – i.e. start playing the next one in your music library

 For an album, tap on this button to view the current queue of songs

 The full range of music controls appears at the bottom of the screen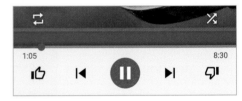

 Drag this button to move through a song

 Tap on this button to shuffle the songs in your collection

Tap on this button to loop the currently queued songs

For music purchased from the Google Play Store, you can tap on these buttons to rate the song

Don't forget

Queued songs are those waiting to be played in the Play Music app.

152

Hot tip

Music controls can also be accessed from the Google Play Music Widget, the Lock screen when music is playing, and the Notification panel when music is playing.

Managing Music

When you are playing music there is still a certain amount of flexibility in terms of managing what is playing, and being scheduled to play. This is known as the music queue. To use this to manage your music:

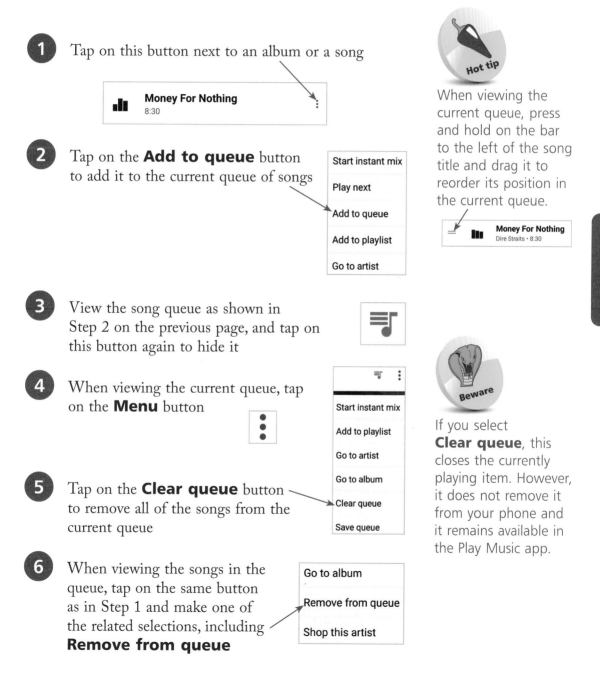

1 Tap on this button next to an album or a song

Money For Nothing
8:30

2 Tap on the **Add to queue** button to add it to the current queue of songs

Start instant mix

Play next

Add to queue

Add to playlist

Go to artist

3 View the song queue as shown in Step 2 on the previous page, and tap on this button again to hide it

4 When viewing the current queue, tap on the **Menu** button

Start instant mix

Add to playlist

Go to artist

Go to album

Clear queue

Save queue

5 Tap on the **Clear queue** button to remove all of the songs from the current queue

6 When viewing the songs in the queue, tap on the same button as in Step 1 and make one of the related selections, including **Remove from queue**

Go to album

Remove from queue

Shop this artist

Hot tip

When viewing the current queue, press and hold on the bar to the left of the song title and drag it to reorder its position in the current queue.

Money For Nothing
Dire Straits • 8:30

153

Beware

If you select **Clear queue**, this closes the currently playing item. However, it does not remove it from your phone and it remains available in the Play Music app.

...cont'd

Pinning music

Music that is bought from the Google Play Store is available for streaming on your phone using your Wi-Fi internet connection. This means that the music is sent from the Google servers, where it is stored, so that it is always backed up and always available.

However, if you are not able to use Wi-Fi, you will probably still want to listen to your music, such as when you are traveling. This can be done by pinning the required music to your phone so that it is physically stored there. To do this:

Items that are not pinned to your device will not be available when you do not have a Wi-Fi connection.

1 Access the Play Music menu and toggle **On** or **Off** the **Downloaded only** button to view the music on your phone that has already

been downloaded to it, rather than just being stored within the Google cloud (i.e. the servers that keep the music that you have bought)

2 For **Downloaded only**, the items that are stored on your phone are shown

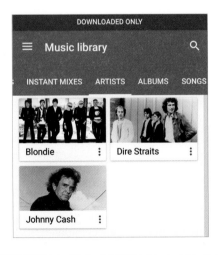

3 The icons next to an item denote its status according to whether it is downloaded to the device or not. A grayed-out button indicates an item that has been bought from the Google Play Store but has not been downloaded to the device. An orange button with a white tick indicates that an item has been downloaded to your phone – i.e. pinned

4 Tap on a grayed-out button so that the pin turns orange, to start the process for downloading and then pinning the item to your phone

The more music that you download to your phone, the more storage space it will take up.

5 The item will be downloaded for storing on your phone. This is indicated in the Notifications bar by the arrow icon

6 Swipe down on the Notifications bar to see the progress of the track(s) being downloaded

Neon Bible - Arcade Fire   16:10
21%

Downloading items over 3G/4G/5G can be expensive, depending on the data plan associated with your Android phone.

7 Tap on an item in Step 6 to view the full download queue

← Manage downloads

712.8 MB
used by Play Music

● OTHER APPS
● PLAY MUSIC
● 6.7 GB FREE

PAUSE DOWNLOADS

Music

Neon Bible
35.6 MB - Arcade Fire

155

Movies and TV Shows

There are different ways in which video content can be viewed on your Android phone:

- Downloading movies and TV shows from the Google Play Store.

- Transferring (uploading) to, or creating your own videos on your phone.

- Watching videos on YouTube.

To obtain movies or TV shows from the Play Store:

Some phones have their own default movies app, which will be linked to the phone manufacturer's own app store. If this is the case, the Play Movies app can still be downloaded from the Play Store, and content can be bought from there.

1 Tap on the **Play Movies & TV** app

2 Tap on the **Library** button on the bottom toolbar to view available content on your phone. This includes movies and TV shows that you have downloaded, and also any recommended titles

3 Tap on an item in the **Library** section to view it

When buying or renting items from the Play Store, there are usually options for doing so in Standard Definition (SD) or High Definition (HD).

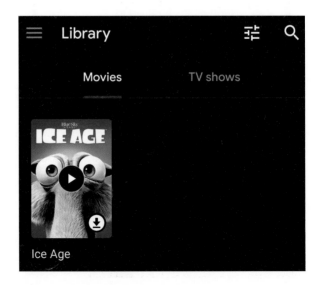

4 Tap on the **Home** button on the bottom toolbar to view the main **Movies & TV** Homepage in the Play Store. This is similar to other Play Store sections for other types of content

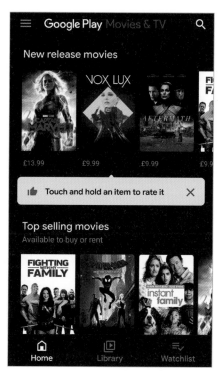

5 Tap on the main panels to view highlighted or recommended movies and TV shows

Tap on the Search icon at the top of the Movies & TV page to search for specific items, using keywords.

6 Tap on an item to view details about it and watch a preview clip of the item

7 Tap on these buttons to buy or rent a movie or TV show. This will be made available within the Play Movies & TV app. (If you rent a movie or a TV show it has to be started within 30 days of being rented, and watched within 48 hours of when it was first started)

If you download movies and TV shows to your phone, they can take up a considerable amount of storage space. Rented items will be automatically deleted once the rental period expires.

Don't forget

Android phones with larger screens are recommended for reading ebooks.

Don't forget

Swipe left and right on a panel on the Shop Homepage to view the items within it.

Hot tip

The Kindle app can be downloaded from the Play Store for reading ebooks. If you already have a Kindle account, your ebooks will be available through the Kindle app on your phone.

Obtaining Ebooks

Due to their size and portability, Android phones are often used for reading ebooks. There is a wide range that can be downloaded from the Play Store, or from the Google Play website, in a similar way to obtaining music, movies and apps.

 Tap on the **Play Books** app (or access the Google Play website)

 Tap on the **Library** button on the bottom toolbar to view your titles. Tap on a cover to open a specific title

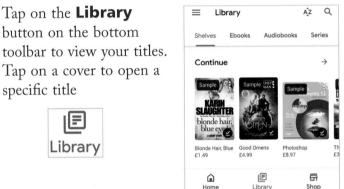

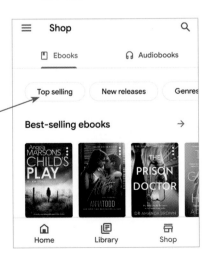

Tap on the **Shop** button on the bottom toolbar

Ebooks can be browsed for and downloaded in a similar way as for other Play Store content. Tap on these buttons to view ebooks according to these headings

Tap on a title to view details about it

6 When you find an ebook you want to read, tap on the **Free Sample** button (if there is one) or the **Ebook** button (with the price)

Good Omens
Neil Gaiman and Terry Pratchett

Random House

Science fiction

FREE SAMPLE | EBOOK £4.99

Hot tip

One of the categories in the Play Store Books section is for **Top free** ebooks. Some classic titles also have free versions if the copyright has expired after a certain period of time following the author's death.

 7 When any ebook from the Play Books store has been downloaded to your phone, it is available within your Play Books library

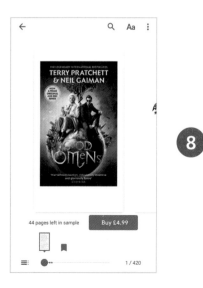

44 pages left in sample | Buy £4.99

1 / 420

 8 Simply select it to open it, and tap in the middle of the page to access the reading controls

Hot tip

Check out the ebook version of this title and other **In Easy Steps** ebooks in the Play Store. Samples for all titles are downloadable for free:

Windows 10 in easy steps
Nick Vandome
In Easy Steps

Computers & technology

FREE SAMPLE | EBOOK £8.97

Around an Ebook

Once you have downloaded ebooks to your phone, you can start reading them. Due to their format there is a certain amount of electronic functionality that is not available in a hard copy version. To find your way around an ebook:

 Swipe left and right on a page to move backwards or forwards by one page

 Tap in the middle of a page to access the reading controls toolbars at the top and bottom of the screen

Search inside   Font size and settings

Settings menu

Return to library   Notes (Table of Contents)

1 / 420

 Drag this button to move through the ebook

 Tap on this button to access the ebook's Table of Contents, bookmarks and notes

 Tap on the **Menu** button to access the specific settings for the title you are reading

 Tap on this button to select text options, including font size and line height

Tap in the top right-hand corner of a page to add a bookmark. A blue bookmark icon appears. Tap again to remove it. Tap on the button in Step 4 to view all bookmarks

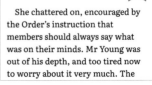
She chattered on, encouraged by the Order's instruction that members should always say what was on their minds. Mr Young was out of his depth, and too tired now to worry about it very much. The

10 Keeping in the Picture

This chapter shows how to make the most of the high-quality cameras that come with most Android phones.

Using Cameras

Most Android phones have their own built-in cameras, which can be used to capture photos directly onto the device. The quality of these varies between makes of phone. Some are good-quality cameras intended to be used for taking photos in a range of conditions; others are mainly for use as a webcam for video calls, or for "selfies" (these are front-facing cameras). To use an Android camera phone:

Hot tip

Use the front-facing camera – i.e. the one on the phone's screen – to take "selfies", which are self-portraits that can also include other people.

1. Tap on the **Camera** app

2. The Camera app displays the current scene, and the control buttons are displayed at the side (landscape view) or at the bottom (portrait view)

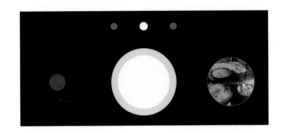

Don't forget

The most recently captured photo is displayed at the right-hand side of the bottom toolbar. Tap on it to open it in the Photos app.

3. Press on the screen to focus the current scene, and tap on this button to take a photo

4. Further controls are available at the top of the screen on the shortcuts bar

Don't forget

Tap on the **Video** button in Step 2 to record a video rather than take a photo.

5. Tap on this button to switch between the front- and rear-facing cameras

6 Tap on the buttons above the shutter button to access different shooting modes and filter options. Tap on one of the options to select that for the next photo

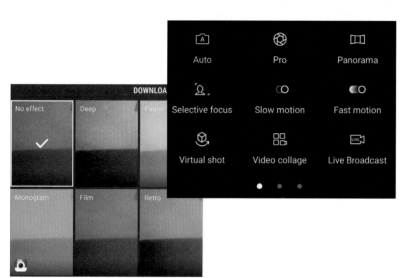

By default, photos captured with the Camera app are displayed in the **Photos** or **Gallery** apps.

Different models of Android phones have their own cameras, which include specific settings and modes. However, the ones listed here will be similar across most Android cameras.

7 Tap on the **Settings** button to view the full range of settings for the camera

8 Tap on one of the items to activate or deactivate it – e.g. the size of photos when they are captured

163

Adding Photos

Android phones are great for storing and, more importantly, displaying your photos. The screen size of most phones is ideal for looking at photos and you can quickly transform it into your own mobile photo album. In addition, it is also possible to share all of your photos in a variety of ways.

Obtaining photos

In addition to capturing photos with your phone, you can obtain them in a number of ways:

- Transferring photos from your computer directly to your phone, via a USB cable (into the **Pictures** folder).

- Transferring photos from your camera to your phone. This is usually done by inserting your camera's memory card into a card reader connected to your computer and then transferring your photos as above.

- Downloading and saving photos from an email, social media, a website or from an internet messaging app.

- Transferring photos from another device via Bluetooth.

Once you have captured or transferred photos to your phone you can then view, edit and share them using the **Photos** (or **Gallery**) app. Photos in the Photos app are stored in different albums, which are created automatically when photos are taken, transferred, or downloaded from an email.

If you keep a lot of photos on your phone this will start to take up storage space.

Personal videos can also be transferred in the same way as with photos. Copy them into the **Videos** folder of your phone. Videos can also be recorded with the video button in the Camera app.

The Photos app is a Google app and is available in the Play Store if it is not pre-installed on a phone.

Downloading from email

Email is a good method of obtaining photos on your phone; other people can send their photos to you in this way, and you can also email your own photos from a computer, a tablet or another mobile device. To use photos from email:

1 Open the email containing the photo and tap on this button to download it

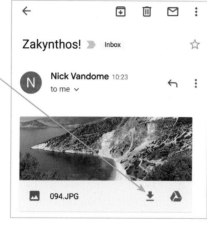

Once the **Download** folder has been created, all other photos downloaded from emails will be placed here.

165

2 The photo will be saved in the **Download** folder within the **Photos** app. This will be automatically created if it is not already there

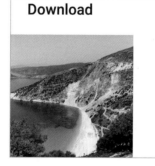

3 Tap on the photo to open the album, and tap on it again to view it at full size in the Photos app. The control buttons are available at the bottom of the screen

Viewing Photos

Once you have obtained photos on your Android phone you can start viewing, managing and editing them.

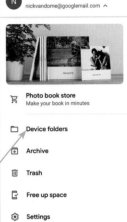

1 Open the **Photos** app and tap on the **Menu** button at the top of the Photos window to view the options

2 Tap on the **Device folders** button from the menu

Don't forget

The default albums in the Photos app are initially empty.

3 Tap on the **Albums** button at the bottom of the screen to view the available albums

Albums

4 Tap on the **Photos** button at the bottom of the screen to view photos that have been taken with the phone

Photos

The photos in the Photos app can be worked with and viewed in different ways:

1 Open the **Photos** app and access the **Photos** section as shown on the previous page

2 The photos and the date on which they were taken are displayed. Tap on a photo to view it at full size

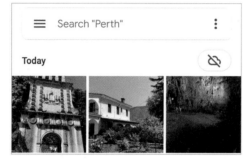

3 In the main window, tap on the **Menu** button and tap on the **Select** button to select individual photos

You can also press and hold on photos to select them.

4 Use the **Menu** button to view the options for working with the images in the folder. This includes selecting items; changing the layout format on the screen to Day, Month or Year view; or creating new items such as a new album

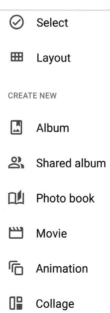

⊘ Select

▦ Layout

CREATE NEW

🖼 Album

👥 Shared album

📖 Photo book

🎬 Movie

🔁 Animation

⬛ Collage

The layout of photos in Step 4 can be in Day, Month or Year view.

...cont'd

Hot tip

Items selected in Step 5 can be shared in a variety of ways by tapping on this button (see page 172 for details).

5 To select items, click on the **Select** button in Step 4 on page 167 and tap on the items you want to select, denoted by a blue circle with a white tick

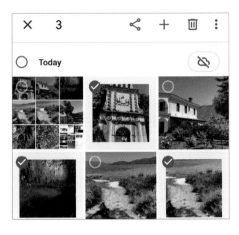

6 Tap on a photo to view it at full size. Tap on this button to access the photo's menu options, or use the bottom toolbar buttons to share, edit, view information, or delete the photo

7 Select options from the photo's menu, including creating a slideshow, adding the photo to an album, using it as a contact photo or wallpaper image (**Use as**), printing the photo, editing the photo or deleting it from the device

Info

Slideshow

Add to album

Use as

Print

Delete from device

Archive

Adding Folders

In addition to the pre-inserted device folders, new ones can be added either from the Photos or the Albums section of the Photos app. To do this:

1 Tap on the **Menu** button

2 Tap on the **Album** button under the **Create New** heading

CREATE NEW

🖼 Album

3 Give the album a name, then tap on the **Select photos** option

←

<u>Summer</u>|

ADD PHOTOS

+   Select photos

4 Tap on the photos to be included in the album and tap on the **Add** button

✕   3   →Add

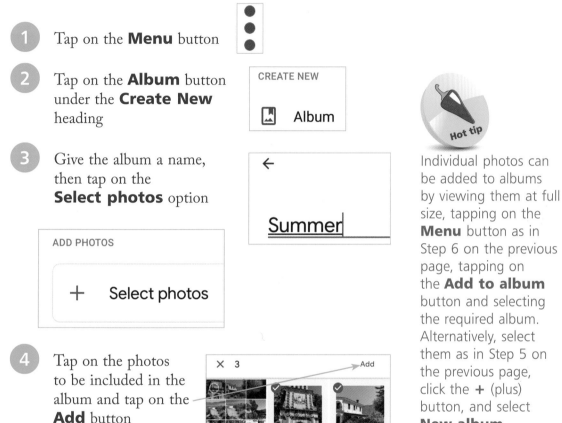

5 The new album is included in the **Albums** section

Summer

Hot tip

Individual photos can be added to albums by viewing them at full size, tapping on the **Menu** button as in Step 6 on the previous page, tapping on the **Add to album** button and selecting the required album. Alternatively, select them as in Step 5 on the previous page, click the **+** (plus) button, and select **New album**.

Editing Photos

Although the Photos app is more for viewing photos, it does have a few editing options so that you can tweak and enhance your images. To access and use these:

Beware

Add small editing changes at a time, otherwise the effect may look too severe.

 Tap on a photo to view it. Tap on this button to access the editing options

Tap on this button on the bottom toolbar to access the filter options. Tap on one of the filters to apply it to the photo

Original   Auto   West

...cont'd

3 Tap on this button to select a range of color-editing functions, including editing the brightness and color contrast of the photo. Drag the sliders to change the effect

4 Tap on this button next to one of the color-editing options to expand it and access sliders for editing elements within the main category

5 To crop a photo, tap on the **Crop** button and drag the resizing handles as required

6 Tap on this button to rotate the photo manually, clockwise or anti-clockwise.
Tap on the **Done** button to finish editing

7 Tap on the **Save copy** button to save any editing changes that have been made

Most photos benefit from some cropping, to give the main subject more prominence.

171

Sharing Photos

It can be great fun and very rewarding to share photos with friends and family. With an Android phone this can be done in several ways:

Social networking sites such as Facebook and Twitter are ideal for sharing photos. Their respective apps can be downloaded from the Play Store, in which case they will also appear as one of the sharing options in Step 2 opposite.

1 Select an album or open an individual photo and tap on the **Share** button

2 Select one of the sharing options. This will be dependent on the apps on your phone, but should include email, messaging, and online storage options such as Google Drive

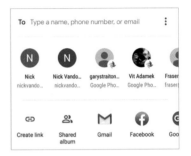

Sharing with Bluetooth

To share with another device using Bluetooth:

Beware

If you are sending photos by Bluetooth, the other device must be paired with your phone, have Bluetooth turned on and accept the request to download the photos when they are sent. When pairing two devices, a password will be created on the first device that then needs to be entered into the second device.

1 Access a photo or make a selection of photos (as shown in Step 5 on page 168), tap on the **Share** button, and then the **Bluetooth** option in Step 2 above

2 If your Bluetooth is not on, turn it **On** in the **Settings** app

3 Select the device with which you want to share your photo(s). These will be sent wirelessly via Bluetooth

11 Online with Chrome

This chapter looks at browser options on Android and also viewing all of your favorite websites with the Chrome browser.

Android Web Browsers

Web browsing is an essential part of our digital world, and on Android phones this functionality can be provided by a variety of web browsers customized for this purpose. They can usually display websites in two ways:

- Optimized for viewing on mobile devices, which are versions that are designed specifically for viewing in this format.

- Full versions of websites (rather than the mobile versions), which are the same as those used on a desktop computer.

Different Android phones have different default browsers but they all have the same general functionality:

- Viewing web pages.

- Bookmarking pages.

- Tabbed browsing – i.e. using tabs to view more than one web page within the same browser window.

If you do not want to use the default browser that is provided with your phone, there is a range of browsers that can be downloaded, for free, from the Play Store.

Enter **browsers for android** into the **Play Store Search box** to view the available options.

Don't forget

Mobile versions of a website usually have **m.** before the rest of the website address – e.g. **m.mysite.com**

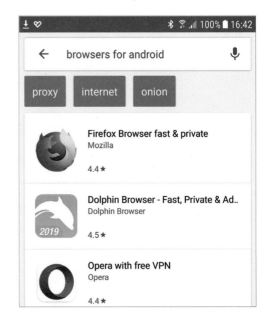

Opening Pages

Web pages can be opened on a phone in an almost identical way as on a desktop computer or laptop. Some Android web browsers display a list of top sites when you open a browser or create a new tab. (The examples on the following pages are for the **Chrome** browser but other browsers operate in a similar way.)

Don't forget

The Chrome browser can be downloaded from the Play Store if it is not already on your phone. This is a Google product and integrates closely with other Google apps on your phone.

 1 The **Search/Address** box can be used to search for keywords or phrases, or you can use it to find specific web pages and sites. Enter text into the **Search/Address** box. If a web address is displayed, tap on it to go directly to that website

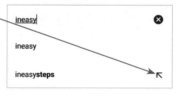

2 Tap on the arrow next to an item to select it in the **Search/Address** box. Tap on the item in the **Search/Address** box to view it

3 For a web address – e.g. one that ends in .com – the web page will be opened; if you have just entered a keyword in the Search/Address box, then the results page will be opened for that keyword. Tap one of the links as required

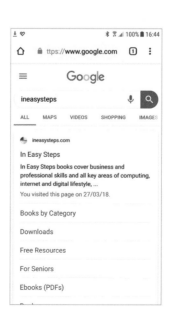

Hot tip

Swipe outwards with your thumb and forefinger on a web page to zoom in on it; pinch inwards to zoom back out. You can double-tap with one finger to zoom in and out too, but this zooms in to a lesser degree than swiping.

Bookmarking Pages

The favorite web pages that you visit can be bookmarked so that you can find them quickly. To do this:

1 Open the page that you want to bookmark and tap on the **Menu** button at the top of the window

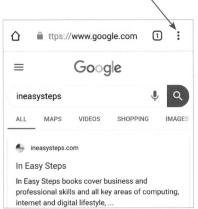

2 Tap on this button to bookmark the page

$\rightarrow$ ★ ⬇ ⓘ ⟳

3 Tap on the button in Step 2 again to edit a bookmark. Tap here in the **Folder** box to specify a folder into which you want to save a bookmark

```
←   Edit bookmark        🗑

Name
In Easy Steps For Seniors - In Easy Steps

Folder
Mobile bookmarks

URL
http://ineasysteps.com/books-by-categc
```

4 Tap on a folder to select it, or tap on the **New folder...** button to create a new folder to use

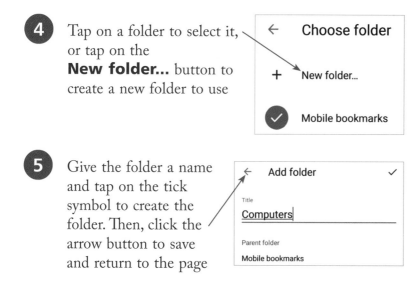

5 Give the folder a name and tap on the tick symbol to create the folder. Then, click the arrow button to save and return to the page

Viewing bookmarks
To view pages that have been bookmarked:

1 To view bookmarks, tap on the **Menu** button and tap on the **Bookmarks** option

2 If folders have been created, tap on one to view its contents

3 Tap on a bookmarked page to open the page in the Chrome browser

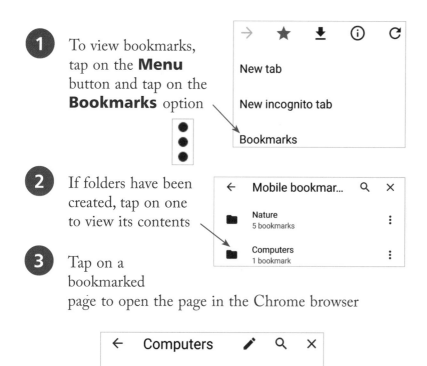

The **Menu** button can also be used to open a new tab. See page 179 for more details about using tabs.

177

Links and Images

Links and images are both essential items on websites; links provide the functionality for moving between pages and sites, while images provide the all-important graphical element. To work with these:

 Tap and hold on a link to access its options (tap once on a link to go directly to the linked page). The options include opening the link in a new tab, opening it in a new tab that does not get recorded by the browser's history (**Open in incognito tab**), copying the web address or link text so that it can be shared with someone or pasted into a document, and downloading the link so that it can be viewed offline

> http://ineasysteps.com/products-page/all_books/photoshop-elements-15-tips-tricks-shortcuts-easy-steps/
>
> Open in new tab
>
> Open in incognito tab
>
> Copy link address
>
> Copy link text
>
> Download link

 Tap and hold on an image to access its options. The options include viewing it on its own (**Open image in new tab**), downloading it, searching Google for the image, or sharing the image

> Open image in new tab
>
> Download image
>
> Search Google for this image
>
> Share image

Using Tabs

Tabs are a common feature on web browsers and allow you to open numerous pages within the same browser window. To do this on an Android phone:

1 Tap on this button at the top right-hand corner of the browser window to view current tabs

ⓘ ineasysteps.com/books ①

The button in Step 1 displays the number of tabs currently open within the Chrome browser.

2 Tap on this button to add a new tab

\+

In Easy Steps

3 Open a new page from the **Search or type web address** box, or any bookmarked pages that are displayed

Google

Search or type web address

In Easy Ste...   Google Play   Google   Google Acc...

Facebook   YouTube   Amazon UK   Argos

179

4 Tap on the button in Step 1 to view all tabs. Tap on a tabbed page to open it. Press and hold on the top of a page and drag it into a different position on the tabs screen

If there are a lot of tabs open, swipe up and down in the tabs window to view them.

5 Tap on the cross on a tab to close it

Don't forget

If the Incognito option is used, web pages will not be stored in the browser history or the search history.

Beware

If children are using your phone, you may not know what they are looking at on the web if they use the Incognito option.

Being Incognito

If you do not want a record to be kept of the web pages that you have visited, most browsers have a function where you can view pages "in private" so that the details are not stored by the browser. In Chrome, this is performed with the Incognito function:

 Tap on the **Menu** button and tap on the **New incognito tab** option

New tab
New incognito tab

 The incognito page opens in a new tab, but any other open tabs are not visible (unless they are incognito too). Open a web page in the same way as for a standard tab

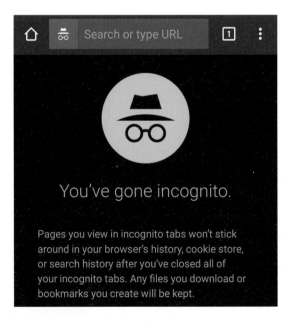

You've gone incognito.

Pages you view in incognito tabs won't stick around in your browser's history, cookie store, or search history after you've closed all of your incognito tabs. Any files you download or bookmarks you create will be kept.

Incognito pages are denoted by this icon at the top left-hand corner of the browser

Browser Settings

Mobile browsers have the usual range of settings that can be accessed from the **Menu** button.

1 Tap on the **Menu** button and tap on the **Settings** option

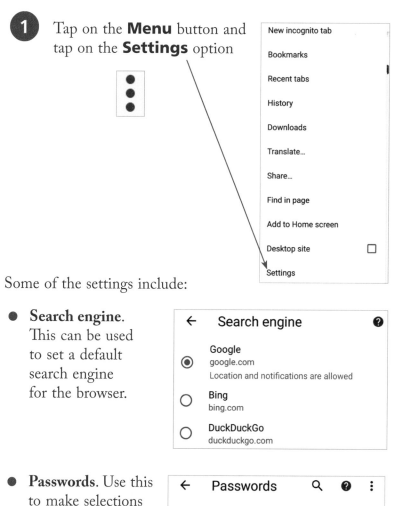

New incognito tab
Bookmarks
Recent tabs
History
Downloads
Translate...
Share...
Find in page
Add to Home screen
Desktop site ☐
Settings

Some of the settings include:

- **Search engine**. This can be used to set a default search engine for the browser.

  ← **Search engine** ❓

  ◉ **Google**
  google.com
  Location and notifications are allowed

  ○ **Bing**
  bing.com

  ○ **DuckDuckGo**
  duckduckgo.com

- **Passwords**. Use this to make selections for how passwords are dealt with by the browser.

  ← **Passwords** 🔍 ❓ ⋮

  Save passwords
  On   ⬤

  Auto Sign-in
  Automatically sign in to websites using stored credentials. When the feature is off, you'll be asked for verification every time before signing in to a website.   ☑

  View and manage saved passwords in your Google Account

Beware

If other people are going to be using your account on your phone, do not turn on the **Auto Sign-in** option for websites in the **Passwords** section.

...cont'd

- Under the **Advanced** heading, tap on the **Privacy** option to specify how your browsing data is used.

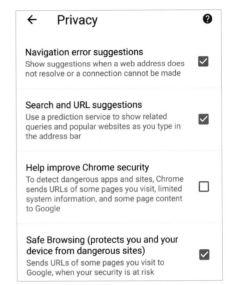

- Under the **Advanced** heading, tap on the **Accessibility** option to specify the text size for viewing web pages.

A cookie is a small piece of data that is stored by the browser, containing information about websites that have been visited.

- Under the **Advanced** heading, tap on the **Site settings** option. Select each option in turn, and then check on or off the options for cookies, JavaScript (which is required to give you full functionality of most websites), and pop-up menus. Tap on the **Location** option to specify whether other websites can use your current location, and the **All sites** option to view settings for individual websites.

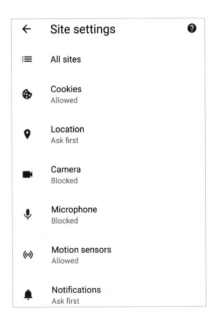

- Under the **Advanced** heading, tap on the **Data Saver** option to specify how web pages are pre-loaded.

12 Staying Secure

This chapter looks at security issues.

Security Issues

Security is a significant issue for all forms of computing, and this is no different for Android phone users. Three of the main areas of concern are:

The world of viruses is a fast-moving one, so it is a good idea to keep up-to-date with the latest viruses that are around. Periodically, search Google for "latest Android viruses" to see what is currently out there.

If young children or grandchildren are borrowing your phone for tasks such as surfing the web or playing games, discuss any restrictions that you have put in place, so they can learn about issues covering online safety.

- **Getting viruses from apps**. Android apps can contain viruses like any other computer programs, but there are antivirus apps that can be used to try to detect viruses. Unlike programs on computers or laptops with file management systems, apps on a phone tend to be more self-contained and do not interact with the rest of the system. This means that if they do contain viruses it is less likely that they will infect the whole phone.

- **Losing your phone or having it stolen**. If your phone is lost or stolen you will want to try to get it back and also lock it remotely so that no-one else can gain access to your data and content. The Google Account web page has an option for finding a lost phone (see page 186), and some antivirus apps also have this option.

- **Restricting access for children**. If you have young children or grandchildren who are using your phone, you will want to know what they are using it for. This is particularly important for the web, social media sites, video-sharing sites and messaging sites where there is the potential to interact with other people. There is also a range of parental control apps that can be downloaded from the Play Store. These can be used to limit access to certain types of apps or content.

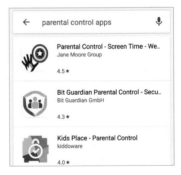

About Antivirus Apps

Android phones are certainly not immune from viruses and malware, and the FBI's Internet Crime Complaint Center (IC3) has even published advice and information about malicious software aimed at Android users. Some general precautions that can be taken to protect your phone are:

- Use an antivirus app on your phone. There are several of these, and they can scan your phone for any existing viruses and also check new apps and email attachments for potential problems.

- Apps that are provided in the Play Store are checked for viruses before they are published, but if you are in any doubt about an app, research it online before you download it. If you do an online search for the app, any issues related to it should be available.

- Do not download any email attachments if you are not sure of their authenticity. If you do not know the person who has sent the email then delete it.

Functionality of antivirus apps

There are several antivirus apps available in the Play Store. Search for **android antivirus apps** (or similar) to view the apps. Most security apps have a similar range of features:

- **Scanning** for viruses and malicious software (malware).

- **Online protection** against malicious software on websites.

- **Anti-theft protection.** This can be used to lock your phone, locate it through Location Services, wipe its contents if they are particularly sensitive, and instruct it to let out an alert sound.

For some of the functions of antivirus and security apps, a sign-in is required.

A lot of antivirus and security apps are free, but there is usually a Pro or Premium version that has to be paid for. It is worth downloading several of the free versions of antivirus apps, to see how you like them and to try out the different functions that they have.

Some antivirus apps also have an option for backing up items such as your contacts, which can then be restored to your phone or another device if they are deleted or corrupted at all.

Locating Your Phone

If you lose your phone or it is stolen, you can try to find its location via the Google Account website.

A lost phone has to be turned on and **Location** enabled in **Settings** > **Connections** for it to be located via the Google Account website.

1 Log in to your online Google Account at: **myaccount.google.com/** and click on the **Find a lost or stolen phone** option under the **Security** tab

Google Account   Q   ⋮   N

personalization   Security   People & sharing

Your devices

Devices that are currently signed in or have been active in your account in the last 28 days

Samsung Galaxy S6
United Kingdom
This device

Find a lost or stolen phone

2 Click on the required device to be located

Samsung Galaxy S6
United Kingdom
THIS DEVICE   >

3 Click on the **Locate** button for the selected device

Samsung Galaxy S6
United Kingdom
This device

☐• Ring

⊙ Locate

4 The device's location is shown on a map. Use the buttons at the bottom of the screen to, from top to bottom: play a sound on the missing phone; lock the phone; or erase all of the data on the phone, if you think it may be compromised

≡ Find My Device   ⚙ N

Needless Rd

The Fish & Chip Company

Harm

Samsung Galaxy S6 ⓘ

Last seen just now

▼ PLUSNET-TXJ5   ↻

🔋 70%

Queen St

Map data ©2019 Terms of Use

☐• PLAY SOUND   >

🔒 SECURE DEVICE   >

🗙 ERASE DEVICE   >

Index